Carol Gilham Jones & Bobbi Finley

FRESH
PERSPECTIVES

Reinventing 18 Classic Quilts
from the International Quilt Study Center & Museum

C&T PUBLISHING

Text copyright © 2012 by Carol Gilham Jones and Bobbi Finley

Contemporary Quilt Photography and Artwork copyright
© 2012 by C&T Publishing, Inc.

Antique Quilts and Quilt Photography copyright
© 2012 by the International Quilt Study Center & Museum

Publisher: Amy Marson

Creative Director: Gailen Runge

Art Director: Kristy Zacharias

Editor: Lynn Koolish

Technical Editors: Alison M. Schmidt and Teresa Stroin

Cover/Book Designer: April Mostek

Production Coordinator: Jenny Davis

Production Editor: S. Michele Fry

Illustrator: Tim Manibusan

Photography by Christina Carty-Francis and Diane Pedersen
of C&T Publishing, Inc., unless otherwise noted

Published by C&T Publishing, Inc., P.O. Box 1456,
Lafayette, CA 94549

Library of Congress Cataloging-in-Publication Data

Jones, Carol Gilham, 1946-

Fresh perspectives : reinventing 18 classic quilts from the International
Quilt Study Center / Carol Gilham Jones and Bobbi Finley.

    pages cm

  ISBN 978-1-60705-431-3 (soft cover)

1. Patchwork--Patterns. 2. Quilting--Patterns. I. Finley, Bobbi, 1936- II.
Title.

TT835.J648 2012

746.46'041--dc23

Printed in China

10 9 8 7 6 5 4 3 2 1

Dedication

From Bobbi to Todd and Kimberly

From Carol to Charles

Acknowledgments

We are extremely grateful to the International Quilt
Study Center & Museum (IQSC&M) at the University
of Nebraska–Lincoln for access to its wonderful collection
of quilts that have served as the inspiration for the project
quilts in this book. Special thanks go to Director Patricia
Crews and to the curator of collections, Carolyn Ducey,
who listened to our ideas for this book and encouraged
us on our way to accomplishing our plan. We appreciate
their willingness to work with C&T Publishing to bring
this book to fruition.

We also want to acknowledge Robert and Ardis James
for their tremendous vision and gift in establishing the
IQSC&M. Ardis passed away in 2011; the IQSC&M
stands as a fitting tribute to her.

We thank the quiltmakers of the past, known and
unknown, whose quilts have inspired us.

The IQSC&M quilts that inspired us also have inspired
our friends, and we offer special thanks to Georgann
Eglinski, Kathe Dougherty, Helen Hodack, Deb
Rowden, and Judy Severson for allowing us to share
their quilts with you in this book. We also thank our
friend Barbara Brackman for the use of her antique quilt
(page 34), for the patterns she provided, and for her con-
tinued generosity in sharing guidance, knowledge, and
fabric.

We thank the whole team at C&T. In particular, we
thank Susanne for shepherding our idea, and Lynn,
Alison, Teresa, April, Tim, Christina, and Diane for
patiently and skillfully making it a reality.

Last, but not least, we are most grateful for the friendship
we have shared over the years and the many collabora-
tions it has inspired.

CONTENTS

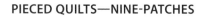

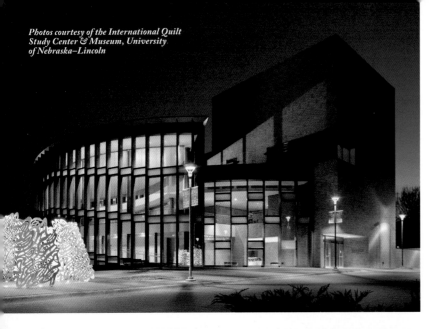

FOREWORD

The International Quilt Study Center & Museum was founded in 1997 when native Nebraskans Ardis and Robert James donated their collection of 1,000 quilts to the University of Nebraska–Lincoln (UNL). Their contribution became the centerpiece of what is now the largest publicly held quilt collection in the world.

Through private funds from the University of Nebraska Foundation and a lead gift from the James family, the center opened in its new location in 2008. The glass-and-brick, environmentally green building houses more than 3,500 quilts, as well as state-of-the-art research and storage space and custom-crafted galleries. The new facility enhances the center's ability to pursue its mission: to collect, preserve, study, exhibit, and promote the discovery of quilts and quiltmaking traditions from many cultures, countries, and times.

The International Quilt Study Center & Museum is an academic program of the Department of Textiles, Clothing, and Design in the College of Education and Human Sciences at UNL. The department offers a unique master's degree in textile history with a quilt studies emphasis, the only program of its kind in the world.

—*International Quilt Study Center & Museum*

INTRODUCTION TO THE INTERNATIONAL QUILT STUDY CENTER & MUSEUM:
A Treasure Trove of Design

Collections

Ardis and Robert James, of Chappaqua, New York, began collecting quilts in 1979. By the time their collection was donated to the University of Nebraska–Lincoln and the International Quilt Study Center & Museum (IQSC&M) was founded, the collection had grown to more than 1,000 quilts.

The James collection is known for its amazing range of both antique and contemporary quilts, dating from the late 1790s to the present, and includes quilts made not only in the United States but also in Europe and Japan. Newly found quilts continue to be added to the collection.

The IQSC&M has expanded its collection since the original James donation, and as the largest publicly held quilt collection in the world, it now also includes:

- The Byron and Sara Rhodes Dillow Collection, including early nineteenth-century antique chintz quilts, eighteenth-century French whitework quilting and wholecloth quilts, Baltimore Album quilts, and rare palampores (printed and painted cotton textiles)

- The Jonathan Holstein Collection, including the 1971 Whitney Museum Exhibition quilts

- The Kathryn Wilson Berenson Collection of French Quilts

- The Linda and Dr. John Carlson Four-Block Quilt Collection

- The Mary Campbell Ghormley Collection of Doll Quilts

- The Robert and Helen Cargo Collection of African-American Quilts

- The Sara Miller Collection of Midwestern Amish Crib Quilts

Exhibits

The galleries at the IQSC&M feature exhibits from the IQSC&M collections as well as other sources. An online exhibit features some of the quilts previously displayed in the galleries.

Online Features

The IQSC&M website (www.quiltstudy.org) offers a wealth of information on the current exhibits and visiting the center as well as future, past, and traveling exhibits. It also has information about the collections and an opportunity to subscribe to the Quilt of the Month to receive in your email inbox every month a photo and information about a quilt selected from the collections. Podcasts are available for viewing or listening to various lectures. But perhaps best of all, there is an online database featuring *thousands* of quilts in an easily searchable format. We spent hours on the website searching the collections to select the eighteen quilts that comprise the projects on the following pages. We hope that one or more of these projects will inspire you. And we encourage you to go to the website to see the treasures that await you there. The IQSC&M is truly a treasure trove of design.

INSPIRATION TO INTERPRETATION:
Classic Quilts as Sources of Inspiration

The eighteen projects in this book are contemporary adaptations that were inspired by antique quilts in the collections of the International Quilt Study Center & Museum. For the makers of the antique quilts, fabric was a principal medium of creative expression; making a quilt also sometimes involved enjoying the companionship of friends. Both are true for us as well. Another point of connection between contemporary quiltmakers and the makers of the antique quilts is an interest in striking design. Because we know that highly developed design has forerunners, we know that the makers of our inspiration quilts learned lessons from the work of their predecessors. We, in turn, can learn valuable design lessons from studying this selection of IQSC&M quilts.

In searching the database of IQSC&M collections for visually interesting quilts, we discovered a wealth of imagination and creativity in quilts of many different aesthetic styles. Thus, the inspiration quilts we chose reflect the broad sweep of our rich and varied quilt heritage. Among the remark- ably diverse quilts we chose are a small Amish quilt made in an improvisational manner, several block-style pieced quilts that exemplify the functional approach to design, a quilt of lively optical effects that is made from rather homely solids, an appliqué quilt featuring exemplary needlework, a chintz masterpiece of fabric ingenuity, a dynamic quilt made principally from feedsacks, and several delightful pictorial quilts.

In interpreting an antique quilt we tried to make a contemporary adaptation that is deeply inspired by the classic quilt and mirrors its essential qualities. In some cases, this meant serving the tradition by adhering very closely to the pattern of the source quilt as we adapted it with contemporary fabrics. In other cases, for the sake of aesthetic impact, our interpretation involved shrinking or enlarging pieces; adding or altering borders; changing overall proportions and/or the quilt shape; changing a medium of expression, for example, from stenciling or embroidery to appliqué; or selecting elements of a quilt and mixing them with elements of our own devising.

Inspired by a beautiful IQSC&M cut-out chintz and appliqué quilt, our friend Judy Severson made a contemporary adaptation that exemplifies the process of interpretation. The essential elements of the antique quilt, which Judy features prominently, are heavy swags that define the perimeter, eight roundels immediately inside the swags, and trefoils on the corners of the medallion.

Cut-Out Chintz Medallion, maker unknown, possibly made in New England, c. 1830–1850, 111″ × 113″, International Quilt Study Center & Museum, University of Nebraska–Lincoln, 1997.007.0454

Inspired Medallion is deeply inspired by the IQSC&M quilt and reflects its essence. Judy preserved the essential elements of the IQSC&M quilt and in her interpretation mixed them with elements of her own devising. She increased the size and decreased the number of appliqué components to make the medallion less fussy. Doing the same thing in the area between the medallion and the swags, she created a much cleaner look. In contrast to her simplifying the central area, Judy amplified the visual interest of the edges of her quilt, thus creating a balanced overall composition. She separated the swags from the borders with small, geometric appliqué motifs and made three borders, rather than one, of varying widths and contrasting values.

A good grounding in traditional designs allows a quiltmaker to expand on what has gone before in ways that reflect her own tastes, interests, and skills. Interpreting an antique quilt by discovering its exceptional elements and building on them may free a quiltmaker from rigid perceptions about fine handiwork and craftsmanship. It may encourage a quiltmaker to value the process at least as much as the product. It may create opportunities for exploring

Inspired Medallion, Judy Severson, Belvedere, California, 2011, 70˝ × 70˝;
machine quilted by Shirley Greenhoe, Thayne, Wyoming, 2011

less mechanistic and more intuitive design strategies. It may lead to being more spontaneous, less predictable.

Building on a fine antique design allows a quiltmaker to develop her own means of expression, to develop design sophistication. It may lead to considering design concepts of symmetry, proportion, and visual complexity achieved with simple means, harmony, and expressive color. And it may help in separating the truly timeless elements of vibrant design from the fashionable taste of the time. Insight into that difference could greatly expand a quiltmaker's design horizon.

For all these reasons, we encourage you to have a go at interpreting an inspirational antique quilt. Start with one of our projects. You may sharpen your design skills. We know you will have a good time, and the windfall of it all is that the processes of selecting and interpreting will link you to the chain of creativity that connects us with past generations.

Bobbi and Carol

HAPPY HOUSES

Bobbi Finley, San José, California, 2010, 70½″ × 70½″;
machine quilted by Holly Casey, King City, California

Schoolhouse, maker unknown, probably made in Oklahoma, c. 1890–1910, 72″ × 78″, International Quilt Study Center & Museum, University of Nebraska–Lincoln, 1997.007.0314

The Inspiration

House quilts are a popular genre for many people, whether simply called "House" or "Schoolhouse." These words conjure up sentimental images: hearth and home, family, and children learning and playing. And perhaps Bobbi's interest in architecture adds to her love of these quilts. The IQSC&M *Schoolhouse* quilt is well designed, with the two red chimneys and the narrow strips defining the roofline and the corner of the building. The houses float on a white background. The alternating blocks of striped fabric add interest. One exhibit catalog stated that the striped fabric might suggest the rows of crops often found in the fields surrounding many country schoolhouses. Whether this was the intent of the maker is, of course, unknown—as is her identity—but it's an appealing idea. Bobbi chose to build her houses with bright, bold contemporary fabrics and to surround them with pale polka dots. She scaled the blocks up to 12″ but included fewer blocks overall. The setting squares with three strips of fabric imply the striped fabric of the original quilt.

Note: This block was designed using BlockBase and Electric Quilt.

Making the Interpretation

FINISHED BLOCK: 12″ × 12″   •   **FINISHED QUILT:** 70½″ × 70½″

FABRIC REQUIREMENTS

Background: 1½ yards for sky, fabric surrounding House blocks, and inner border

Polka dot: ½ yard for house doors and windows

Brights: Minimum of 25 fat quarters if some setting square fabrics are used for houses; maximum of 36 if no repeats

Striped border: 2¼ yards

Batting: 78″ × 78″

Backing: 4½ yards

Binding: ⅜ yard for ¼″-wide single-fold straight-grain binding

CUTTING

See template patterns on pages 15–17.

Background:

Cut 13 Template A.

Cut 13 Template C.

Cut 13 Template L.

Cut 13 Template D.

Cut 26 rectangles 1½″ × 10½″.

Cut 26 rectangles 1½″ × 12½″.

Cut 7 strips 1½″ × width of fabric for inner border.

Polka dot:

Cut 13 Template J and 26 Template R from the same fabric for all the doors and windows.

Brights:

Cut 3 rectangles 4½″ × 12½″ from each of 12 different fat quarters for the setting squares, for a total of 36 rectangles.

Cut 1 each using Templates F, G, K, O, N, and P and 2 each of Templates B, Q, and I for each house. Cut for 13 houses.

Templates E, H, and M define the roofline and corner of the building. Use the same fabric for these 3 templates in each of the houses, cutting 1 from each template for each of the 13 houses. If you want to use the same fabric for all of the houses, cut 13 each from Templates E, H, and M.

Be sure to mark the top of Templates P and N because they will not fit properly if not oriented correctly. You may also want to mark the point where seamlines intersect.

Striped border:

Cut 4 strips 4½″ × length of fabric for outer border.

Binding:

Cut 8 strips 1¼″ × width of fabric.

TIP

As you make your fabric selections for each House block, audition the fabrics and perhaps fussy cut to capture a particular portion of the fabric, but be sure to align the template edges with the straight grain of the fabric to avoid stretchy bias edges.

Construction

House Blocks

Using the house diagram as a guide, assemble the blocks in sections and units. Press as needed.

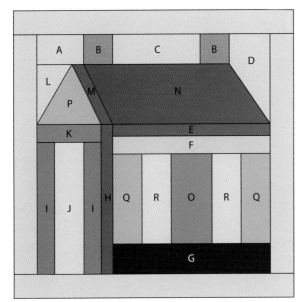

House diagram

1. Sew A to B to C; then add another B to create Unit 1.

2. Sew L to P to M to N to create Unit 2. Be sure to align the pieces in the right direction.

3. Sew Unit 1 to Unit 2 to create the roof section.

4. Sew D to B, starting at the top and stopping ¼″ from the edge of fabric at the corner. Then stitch the rest of D to N, starting at the place where the previous seam stopped, to complete the roof section.

5. Sew an I to each side of J; then sew K to one end (the top) and then H to the right side. This is the door, Unit 3.

6. Sew E to F. E is the top. This is Unit 4.

7. Sew together a Q and an R. Repeat with another Q and R. Then sew the R sides to O. Sew G to one side (the bottom) and the F side of Unit 4 to the other side.

8. Sew the unit from Step 7 to H on Unit 3.

9. Sew the unit from Step 8 to the roof section for a completed house.

10. Sew 1½″ × 10½″ background rectangles to both sides of each completed house.

11. Sew 1½″ × 12½″ background rectangles to the top and bottom of each completed house.

Setting Squares

Sew 3 different bright rectangles 4½″ × 12½″ together to form a 12½″ × 12½″ square. Press. Make 12 setting squares.

Assembly

1. Arrange alternating House blocks and setting squares in 5 rows of 5 with a House block at the beginning and end of the first, third, and fifth rows.

2. Sew the blocks together in rows. Press.

3. Sew the rows together. Press.

TIP

Pressing the seam allowances of alternating rows of blocks in opposite directions will reduce bulk.

Inner Border

1. Sew together the 1½″ background strips to form 2 strips 60½″ long and 2 strips 62½″ long. Press.

2. Measure the assembled top and adjust the strip length if necessary.

3. Sew the 60½″ strips to the sides, and then sew the 62½″ strips to the top and bottom. Press.

Outer Border

Note: *The striped pattern of the border fabric begs for a mitered border so that the lines continue around the corner without interrupting the visual impact. The following instructions are for a mitered border. Depending on your border fabric, you may wish to place the borders in the more usual fashion of 2 strips even with each side and then strips across the top and bottom. Be sure to measure carefully and cut your strips accordingly if you choose the butted border style.*

1. Pin the center of each side of the quilt top to the center of each border piece; then pin the entire border in place.

2. Sew, starting and stopping the stitching ¼″ from the quilt edge.

3. Press the borders open.

4. For each corner, fold 1 border strip under so it meets the edge of the adjoining strip and forms a 45° angle. Be sure the edges are aligned on each side.

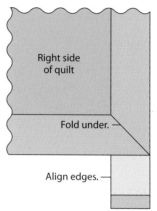

Fold border under adjacent border strip at 45° angle.

5. Firmly press the mitered fold in place.

6. Fold the quilt top diagonally from the corner, right sides together, and again align the long edges of the border strips. Draw a line on the pressed crease line. Pin across the drawn line. Beginning at the inside corner, backstitch, stitch on the drawn line to the outside edge, and backstitch again.

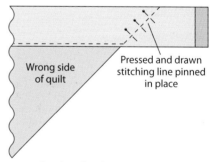

Stitching line for mitered corner

7. Turn the quilt top to the right side; if all is well, trim off the excess fabric to a ¼″ seam allowance and press the seam open.

Finishing

1. Layer and baste the quilt.

2. Quilt as desired.

3. Bind.

House Block Templates

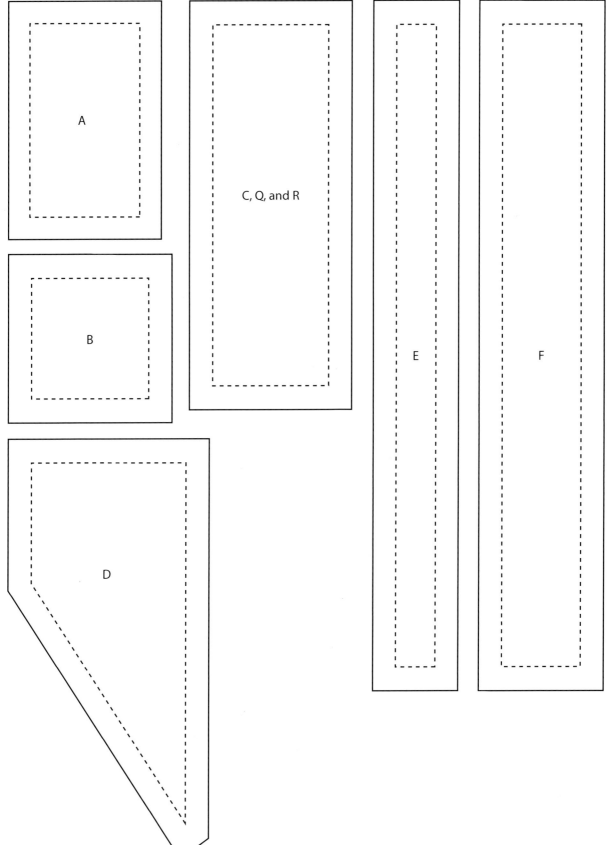

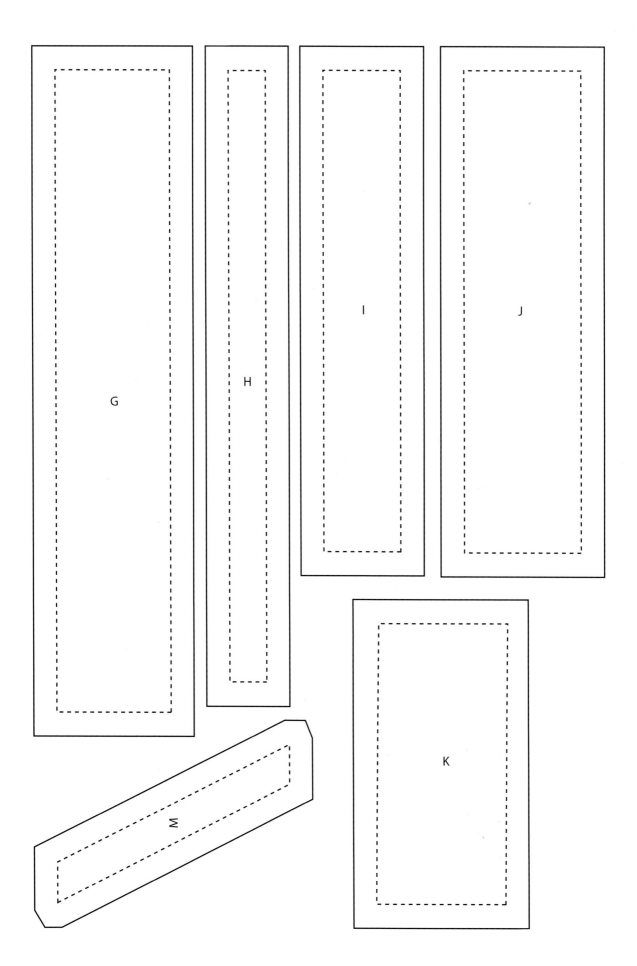

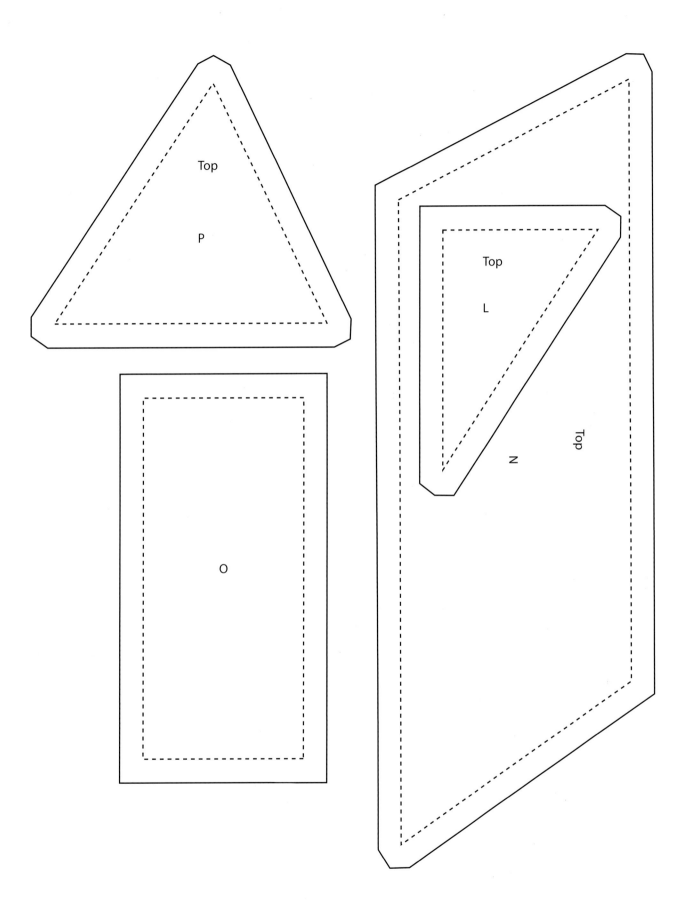

Top

P

O

Top

L

N

Top

POSTAGE STAMP BASKETS

Bobbi Finley, San José, California, 2010, 53″ × 53″;
machine quilted by Holly Casey, King City, California

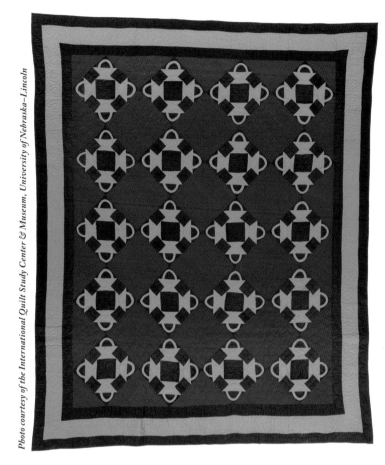

Baskets, made by a member of the Old Order River Brethren in Chambersburg, Pennsylvania, c. 1900, 72″ × 84″, International Quilt Study Center & Museum, University of Nebraska–Lincoln, 2009.039.0023

The Inspiration

Basket quilts are popular with quiltmakers, and this particular basket quilt was a favorite of Robert and Ardis James. The fabric and color choices along with the design formations found in this quilt suggest a typical Amish quilt, and the maker was from a related religious group. This basket design is now known as Postage Stamp Basket after the design of a stamp issued by the U.S. Postal Service in 1978 to commemorate Folk Art USA: Quilts.

We wanted to include a basket pattern quilt, and Bobbi chose this particular one because the bold colors and the symmetry of the four simple baskets set with the handles facing outward attracted her attention. Generally, four basket blocks are set with the handles facing inward, but reversing the blocks adds interest with the handles forming a circle for the eye to follow and leaves a square in the center to show off fabric or quilting. Also, setting the basket blocks on

point with setting squares in between adds to the visual interest. Rather than choosing solid colors as in the inspiration quilt, Bobbi selected a floral fabric to use as a focus in the setting squares. However, the design and colors of the flowers in this fabric would never be found in nature. From the colors in this focus fabric, Bobbi selected fabrics for the baskets that include a paisley and other graphic patterns. She included fewer blocks, which scales down the size of the quilt. She retained the border treatment of the inspiration quilt.

This is a puzzle card made of Folk Art USA: Quilts postage stamps from Bobbi's collection.

Making the Interpretation

FINISHED BLOCK: 10″ × 10″ (4 basket units)

FINISHED QUILT: 53″ × 53″

FABRIC REQUIREMENTS

Basket blocks: 8 or more dark and at least 3 light fat quarters, or 6–8 light fat quarters for a more scrappy look

Focus fabric: 1½ yards for setting squares, triangles, and center border

Light: 1½ yards for inner and outer border—should contrast with focus fabric

Backing: 3½ yards

Batting: 60″ × 60″

Binding: ⅓ yard for ¼″-wide single-fold straight-grain binding

CUTTING

36 baskets are needed; cutting instructions below are for 1 basket.

BASKET BLOCKS:

Basket (dark) fabric:
Cut 1 square 4⅜″ × 4⅜″; cut the square in half diagonally. From one of the resulting triangles, cut a 1″-wide bias strip from the long side, and discard the rest of that triangle.

Cut 1 square 2⅜″ × 2⅜″; cut the square in half diagonally.

Background (light) fabric:
Cut 1 square 4⅜ × 4⅜″; cut the square in half diagonally. You will use only 1 of the resulting triangles. Save the other for another Basket block.

Cut 1 square 2⅜″ × 2⅜″; cut the square in half diagonally.

Cut 1 square 2″ × 2″.

Cut 2 rectangles 2″ × 2½″.

SETTING SQUARES, TRIANGLES, AND BORDERS:

Focus fabric:
On the lengthwise grain, cut 2 strips 3½″ × 45″ and 2 strips 3½″ × 51″ for center borders.

From the remaining fabric:

Cut 4 squares 10½″ × 10½″.

Cut 2 squares 15⅜″ × 15⅜″; cut the squares in half diagonally twice for side triangles.

Cut 2 squares 8″ × 8″; cut the squares in half diagonally for corner triangles.

Light:
On the lengthwise grain, cut 2 strips 1½″ × 43″ and 2 strips 1½″ × 45″ for inner borders.

On the lengthwise grain, cut 2 strips 1½″ × 51″ and 2 strips 1½″ × 53″ for outer borders.

BINDING:

Cut 6 strips 1¼″ × width of fabric.

Construction

Baskets

Bobbi is indebted to Alex Anderson's instructions for piecing Basket blocks in her book Quilts for Fabric Lovers *(page 32), C&T Publishing, 1994.*

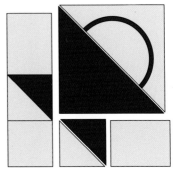

Postage Stamp Basket unit; make 36.

1. Staystitch ⅛″ from the bias edge of the large background triangle.

2. For the handle, fold the 1″-wide bias strip (cut from one of the large triangles of the basket fabric) in half lengthwise, wrong sides together.

3. Arrange the handle on the staystitched background triangle using the handle placement illustration (page 21) as a reference. The folded edge should be toward the stay stitching and the raw edges toward the corner. Be sure to place the longer side of the folded bias handle facedown on the right side of the background triangle.

4. Pin the handle in place; then hand or machine stitch with a ¼″ seam allowance.

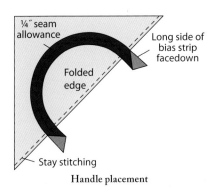

¼″ seam allowance

Long side of bias strip facedown

Folded edge

Stay stitching

Handle placement

5. Flip the basket handle up over the stitched edge and whipstitch the outside folded edge down. Trim the handle ends even with the edge of the triangle.

6. Sew the triangle with the handle to the basket fabric large triangle. Press toward the basket.

7. Sew the small background triangles to the small basket fabric triangles to form 2 half-square triangle squares, each 2″ × 2″. Press.

8. Sew the basket side of each of these squares to the short end of a background rectangle. Press. Make 2.

9. Sew 1 of these strips to a side of the basket/handle unit. Press.

10. Sew the 2″ × 2″ background square to the background triangle on the remaining strip. Press.

11. Sew this to the other side of the basket/handle unit to complete the basket. Press.

12. Sew 4 baskets together with the handles to the outside of the resulting square, taking care to match the basket points. Press.

Assembly

1. Arrange the triangles, setting squares, and basket squares together in diagonal rows as shown.

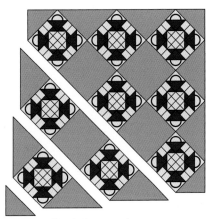

Block placement diagram

2. Sew everything together in diagonal rows. Press.

3. Sew the diagonal rows together, and press.

TIP

Pressing the seam allowances in one row of blocks in the opposite direction from those in the next row of blocks will reduce bulk.

Borders

1. Sew a 1½″ × 43″ inner border strip to each side. Press.

2. Sew a 1½″ × 45″ inner border strip to the top and another to the bottom. Press.

3. Sew a 3½″ × 45″ center border strip to each side. Press.

4. Sew a 3½″ × 51″ center border strip to the top and and another to the bottom. Press.

5. Sew a 1½″ × 51″ outer border strip to each side. Press.

6. Sew a 1½″ × 53″ outer border strip to the top and and another to the bottom. Press.

Finishing

1. Layer and baste the quilt.

2. Quilt as desired.

3. Bind.

LONG-STEMMED
JAPANESE ROSES

Carol Gilham Jones, Lawrence, Kansas, 2010, 91″ × 91″;
machine quilted by Lori Kukuk, McLouth, Kansas

Nine-Patch Variation,
maker unknown,
probably made in
Lancaster County,
Pennsylvania,
c. 1840–1850,
75″ × 88″,
International Quilt
Study Center
& Museum,
University of
Nebraska–Lincoln,
2006.043.0105

The Inspiration

Carol was fascinated by the photo of this unusual mid-nineteenth-century quilt in the IQSC&M online database. She saw geometric flowers perched on long stems—the squares formed by light fabrics in Irregular Nine-Patch blocks on stems of vertical lines formed by light fabrics in Double Four-Patch blocks. Other Nine-Patch, Four-Patch, and Double Four-Patch blocks in medium and dark values tend to blend, even disappear, into the zigzags of the dark chintz between the on-point blocks. The pale "flowers" punctuate the dark, dense pattern. Carol's interpretation puts even more emphasis on the flowers by lengthening the stems, pulling them in both directions, and increasing the ratio of flower blocks to blocks that are closer in value to the zigzags.

Intending to re-create the pale flower accents, Carol chose a dark Japanese print with stylized roses in subdued grays, greens, and blues for the zigzags. The subtle tones of the printed roses are repeated in the medium-value fabrics she chose for the blocks, and some Asian motifs—waves, calligraphy, and chrysanthemums—appear in the light- and medium-value prints. She put punch in the somber palette by including bright, clear reds in the blocks and binding.

Making the Interpretation

FINISHED BLOCK: 8″ × 8″ • FINISHED QUILT: 91″ × 91″

FABRIC REQUIREMENTS

Note: *To heighten the pattern and textural interest in this quilt, Carol used quite a variety of fabrics—10 lights; 18 medium blues, gray-blues, and gray-greens; and 8 reds.*

Lights: A variety of fabrics to total 1½ yards for Nine-Patches and Four-Patches

Mediums: A variety of fabrics to total 2¾ yards for Nine-Patches and Four-Patches

Reds: A variety of fabrics to total 1½ yards for Nine-Patches and Four-Patches

Background: 4 yards

Backing: 8½ yards

Batting: 98″ × 98″

Binding: ½ yard for ¼″-wide single-fold straight-grain binding

CUTTING

Lights:

Cut 64 rectangles 2½″ × 4½″.

Cut 104 squares 2½″ × 2½″.

Mediums:

Cut 110 squares 4½″ × 4½″.

Cut 184 squares 2½″ × 2½″.

Reds:

Cut 32 squares 4½″ × 4½″.

Cut 104 squares 2½″ × 2½″.

Background:

Cut 30 squares 12⅝″ × 12⅝″; cut squares in half diagonally twice for setting triangles.

Cut 8 squares 6⅝″ × 6⅝″; cut squares in half diagonally once for corner triangles.

Binding:

Cut 10 strips 1¼″ × width of fabric.

Construction

Red-and-Light Irregular Nine-Patch Blocks

Sew red squares and light rectangles together as shown to make 8 Irregular Nine-Patch blocks. Press.

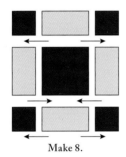

Make 8.

Medium-and-Light Irregular Nine-Patch Blocks

Sew medium-value squares and light rectangles together as shown above to make 8 Irregular Nine-Patch blocks. Press.

Red-and-Medium Four-Patch Blocks

Sew 2 red 4½″ × 4½″ squares and 2 medium-value 4½″ × 4½″ squares together as shown to make 5 Four-Patch blocks. Press.

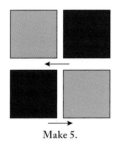

Make 5.

Medium-Value Four-Patch Blocks

Sew together 2 pairs of medium-value 4½″ × 4½″ squares as shown above to make 6 Four-Patch blocks. Press.

Double Four-Patch Blocks

1. Sew together 2 light 2½″ × 2½″ squares and 2 red or medium-value 2½″ × 2½″ squares to make 52 Four-Patches. Press.

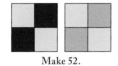

Make 52.

Note: *Keep the placement of lights consistent. Otherwise, mix and match reds and medium values for a variety of interesting Double Four-Patch blocks.*

2. Sew the remaining 2½″ × 2½″ squares together in pairs to make a total of 30 Four-Patches. Press.

3. Sew together 2 red or medium-value 4½″ × 4½″ squares of the same fabric and 2 Four-Patches that match each other to make a Double Four-Patch block. Press. Make 41.

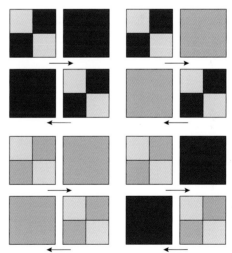

Double Four-Patch block combinations

Assembly

1. Arrange the Nine-Patch, Four-Patch, and Double Four-Patch blocks in columns as shown.

Arrange blocks in columns. Note placement of light-value squares.

TIP

Pressing the seam allowances of alternating diagonal strips in opposite directions will reduce bulk.

2. Sew a setting triangle to the lower left and upper right side of every block to make diagonal strips except as follows: In columns A, C, E, and G, sew corner triangles (instead of side triangles) to the top sides of the top block and to the bottom sides of the bottom block. In columns, B, D, F, and H, do not sew any triangles to the top sides of the top block or to the bottom sides of the bottom block. Press.

3. Sew the diagonal strips together to make columns.

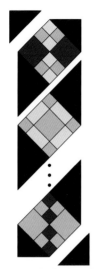

Columns A, C, E, and G   Columns B, D, F, and H

4. Sew the columns together. Press.

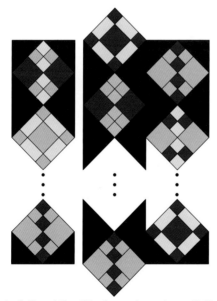

Columns A, C, E, and G will be shorter than columns B, D, F, and H.
When sewing them together, position the longer columns so that half of the top and
bottom blocks extend beyond the top and bottom of the shorter columns.

5. Trim columns B, D, F, and H so that they are even with the other columns.

1. Layer and baste.

2. Quilt as desired.

3. Bind.

MORRIS TAPESTRY NINE-PATCH

Carol Gilham Jones, Lawrence, Kansas, 2010, 89¾″ × 89¾″;
machine quilted by Lori Kukuk, McLouth, Kansas

Nine-Patch Variation, Jane Gibb, possibly made in Quincy, Illinois, c. 1835, 97″ × 103″, International Quilt Study Center & Museum, University of Nebraska–Lincoln, 1997.007.0575

The Inspiration

We love the dancing patterns of lights and darks that Jane Gibb created by alternating light- and dark-centered Irregular Nine-Patch blocks. Setting her blocks on point makes Gibb's quilt appear even more lively than it would if constructed on horizontal and vertical lines.

By increasing the size of the Irregular Nine-Patch blocks, Carol made this pattern a showcase for some large-scale stripes and other printed motifs in William Morris reproduction fabrics by Barbara Brackman. Carol modified the borders for a more unified overall look.

Making the Interpretation

FINISHED BLOCK: 9″ × 9″

FINISHED QUILT: 89¾″ × 89¾″

FABRIC REQUIREMENTS

Note: For a scrappy look, you will need approximately 12 to 15 darks and an equal number of lights.

Lights: A variety of fabrics to total 2¾ yards for Nine-Patches

Darks: A variety of fabrics to total 2¾ yards for Nine-Patches

Setting squares: 1¾ yards

Side and corner triangles: 1⅜ yards

Backing: 8½ yards

Batting: 97″ × 97″

Binding: ½ yard for ¼″-wide single-fold straight-grain binding

DESIGN TIP

Using the setting-square and triangle fabrics in some of the Nine-Patch blocks that are not adjacent to the borders will help blend the borders and the Nine-Patch blocks for an integrated overall look.

Darks:

Cut 25 squares 5½″ × 5½″.

Cut 100 squares 2½″ × 2½″.

Cut 144 rectangles 2½″ × 5½″.

Lights:

Cut 36 squares 5½″ × 5½″.

Cut 144 squares 2½″ × 2½″.

Cut 100 rectangles 2½″ × 5½″.

Setting squares:

Cut 24 squares 9½″ × 9½″.

Side and corner triangles:

Cut 6 squares 14″ × 14″; cut squares in half diagonally twice for side triangles.

Cut 2 squares 7¼″ × 7¼″; cut squares in half diagonally once for corner triangles.

Binding:

Cut 10 strips 1¼″ × width of fabric.

Construction

Irregular Nine-Patch Blocks

Sew light and dark squares and rectangles together as shown to make 61 Irregular Nine-Patch blocks. Press.

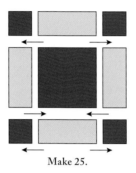
Make 25.

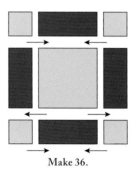
Make 36.

Assembly

1. Sew the triangles, setting squares, and Irregular Nine-Patch blocks together in diagonal rows as shown; then press.

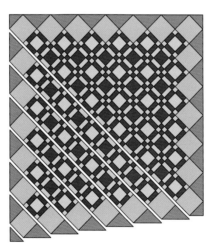
Sew into diagonal rows.

2. Sew the diagonal rows together; then press.

TIP

Pressing the seam allowances of alternating rows of blocks in opposite directions will reduce bulk.

Finishing

1. Layer and baste.

2. Quilt. The large squares of the Irregular Nine-Patch blocks offer an opportunity for some beautiful quilting.

3. Bind.

ANOTHER INTERPRETATION

Park Avenue Nine-Patch, Bobbi Finley, San José, California, 2010, 61˝ × 61˝;
machine quilted by Holly Casey, King City, California

Bobbi, too, made a quilt inspired by Jane Gibb's *Nine-Patch Variation*. Bobbi chose the rich colors of Moda's Park Avenue collection of fabrics designed by 3 Sisters and retained the border treatment of the nineteenth-century quilt.

NINE-PATCH RHYTHMS

Bobbi Finley, San José, California, and Carol Gilham Jones,
Lawrence, Kansas, 2011, 53¾″ × 53¾″; machine quilted by Shirley Greenhoe, Thayne, Wyoming

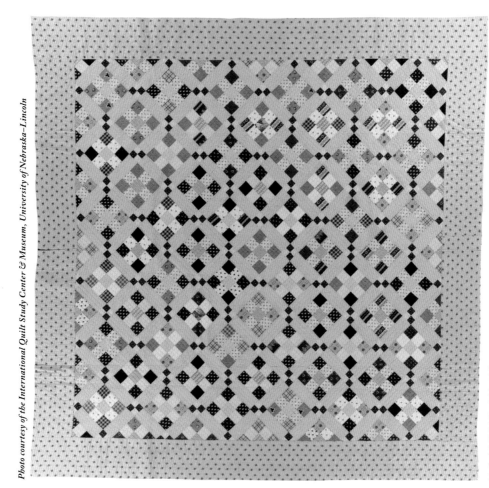

Nine-Patch, made by Mrs. Eshleman, probably in Lancaster County, Pennsylvania, c. 1860, 90″ × 92″, International Quilt Study Center & Museum, University of Nebraska–Lincoln, 1997.007.0647

The Inspiration

Nine-Patch quilts in all their various formations provide a never-ending source of inspiration and design. They are popular with quiltmakers for their simplicity and ease of piecing with no triangles or curves, just straight seams. The simple design of the equal Nine-Patch in the inspiration quilt selected here is a pleasing example accomplished by surrounding the Nine-Patches with yellow sashing and adding the Four-Patch cornerstones. In addition, the four dark corners of the Nine-Patches with pink centers and inner light squares add interest and balance. A secondary pattern is created by setting the Four-Patch cornerstones in two directions. Much of the visual interest is accomplished by the fact that Mrs. Eshleman set her blocks on point. As a comparison, the antique Nine-Patch on page 34 uses the same block format but is set in straight rows.

Antique Nine-Patch quilt top set in straight rows, maker and date unknown; collection of Barbara Brackman

As much as we admired the simple pastel prints of the Eshleman quilt, it did invite interpretation in contemporary fabrics. This collaboration took off when Carol contributed the batiks for the sashing strips and the wavy stripe for the setting triangles to Bobbi's stack of fat quarters. Bobbi's fabrics, including the flowery border print, are all from one fabric line. The additional fabrics added variety and altered the sameness that sometimes occurs when using just one fabric line in a quilt. All the wavy stripes in the setting triangles are set vertically to add even more directionality to the quilt.

Making the Interpretation

FINISHED NINE-PATCH BLOCK: *6″ × 6″* • FINISHED QUILT: *53¾″ × 53¾″*

FABRIC REQUIREMENTS

Lights (white, beige, pink, green):
4–6 fat quarters for Nine-Patches

Darks (green, burgundy):
4–6 fat quarters for Nine-Patches

Mediums (green, burgundy):
2–3 fat quarters for Nine-Patches

Pink print: ¼ yard for Four-Patches

Burgundy print: ¼ yard
for Four-Patches

Sashing: 1 yard

Setting triangles: ½ yard

Border: 1⅜ yards

Backing: 3⅔ yards

Batting: 61″ × 61″

Binding: ⅓ yard for ¼″-wide single-
fold straight-grain binding

CUTTING

Lights: Cut 100 light
squares 2½″ × 2½″.

Darks: Cut 100 dark squares 2½″ × 2½″.

Mediums: Cut 25 medium
squares 2½″ × 2½″.

Pink print: Cut 2 strips 1½″ × width
of fabric. Cut 1 strip 2½″ by 22″.

Burgundy print: Cut 2
strips 1½″ × width of fabric.
Cut 1 strip 2½″ by 22″.

Sashing: Cut 64 rectangles 2½″ × 6½″.

Setting triangles: Cut 3 squares
9¾″ × 9¾″; cut squares in half diagonally twice for side triangles. Cut 2
squares 5⅛″ × 5⅛″; cut squares in half
diagonally once for corner triangles.

Borders: Cut 4 strips 4½″ × 45¾″
along the *lengthwise* grain.

Binding: Cut 6 strips
1¼″ × width of fabric.

Construction

Nine-Patches

Arrange 4 dark, 4 light, and 1 medium 2½″ × 2½″ squares as shown. Sew in rows, and then sew the 3 rows together. Press. Make 25.

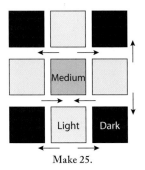

Make 25.

Four-Patches

1. Sew a 1½″ pink strip to a 1½″ burgundy strip lengthwise. Press to the burgundy side. Make 2. Cut into 1½″ × 2½″ segments.

Make 2.

2. Sew 2 segments together with same color on the diagonal. Make 40. Press.

Make 40.

3. Sew the 2½″ pink strip to the 2½″ burgundy strip lengthwise. Press to the burgundy side and then cut 8 segments 2½″ × 4½″.

4. Sew 2 segments together with same color on the diagonal. Make 4. Press.

• • • *Fresh Perspectives* • • •

Assembly

Quilt Center

1. Arrange the Nine-Patches, small Four-Patches, sashing rectangles, and setting triangles in diagonal rows as shown. When pleased with the arrangement, sew together into diagonal rows. Press.

TIPS

• Pressing the seam allowances of alternating rows of blocks in opposite directions will reduce bulk.

• Be sure to place the Four-Patches so that the vertical and horizontal lines are maintained by the color placement.

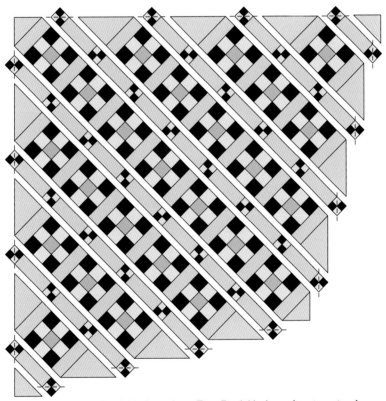

Sew together Nine-Patch blocks, sashing, Four-Patch blocks, and setting triangles.

2. Sew the diagonal rows together. Press.

3. Trim off the small Four-Patches even with the outside edge of the quilt.

Borders

1. Sew border strips to opposite sides of the quilt.

2. Sew the 4½″ × 4½″ Four-Patches to the ends of the 2 remaining border strips, placing the pink squares so that they will be on the outside corners of the quilt. Press. Sew these strips to the remaining 2 sides of the quilt. Press.

Finishing

1. Layer and baste the quilt.

2. Quilt as desired.

3. Bind.

INDIGO NINE-PATCH

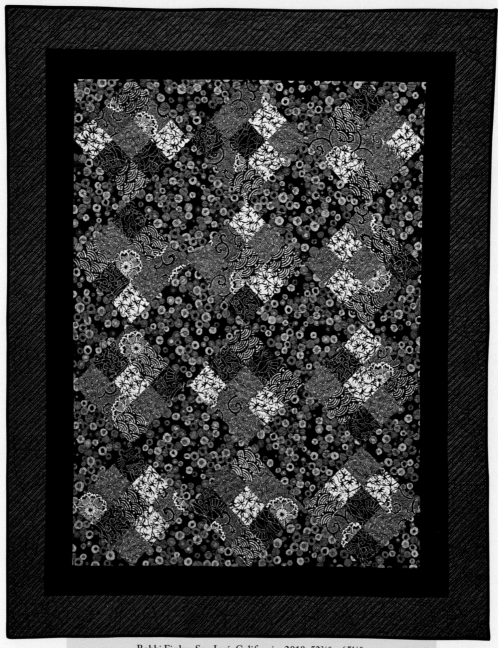

Bobbi Finley, San José, California, 2010, 52¾″ × 65½″;
machine quilted by Holly Casey, King City, California

Nine Patch, maker unknown, possibly made in Arthur, Illinois, c. 1900–1920, 34″ × 41″, International Quilt Study Center & Museum, University of Nebraska–Lincoln, 2000.007.0045

The Inspiration

We love the simplicity of this charming Amish crib quilt with its typical Amish colors set with the usual wide borders that show off the beautiful quilting the Amish are known for. It is one of many crib quilts in the Sarah Miller Collection of the IQSC&M.

When Bobbi stumbled upon a fabulous collection of Japanese indigo prints, she put aside the bold colors of the inspiration quilt to make her interpretation. She used a related Japanese print of dotted circles to add a little subdued color and soften the stronger geometrics of the indigo prints. She maintained the twelve blocks and rectangular shape of the inspiration quilt and the relative size of the two borders, but to show off the fabric designs she increased the size of the Nine-Patches and the setting squares for an overall larger quilt.

Making the Interpretation

FINISHED BLOCK: 9″ × 9″ • **FINISHED QUILT:** 52¾″ × 65½″

FABRIC REQUIREMENTS

Fabrics for the Nine-Patch blocks should have a range of patterns and value for contrast.

Indigo prints: 5 or more fat quarters for Nine-Patch blocks

Japanese print: 1⅜ yards for setting squares and triangles

Indigo solid: 1½ yards for inner border

Blue geometric print: 1⅔ yards for outer border

Backing: 3½ yards

Batting: 60″ × 73″

Binding: ⅓ yard for ¼″-wide single-fold straight-grain binding

CUTTING

Indigo prints:

Cut 108 squares 3½″ × 3½″.

Japanese print:

Cut 6 squares 9½″ × 9½″ for setting squares.

Cut 3 squares 14″ × 14″; cut squares in half diagonally twice for side setting triangles. (This will provide 12 triangles. You will use 10.)

Cut 2 squares 7¼″ × 7¼″; cut squares in half diagonally once for corner setting triangles.

Indigo solid:

Cut 2 strips 3½″ × 51½″ and 2 strips 3½″ × 44¾″ on the lengthwise grain.

Blue geometric print:

Cut 2 strips 4½″ × 57½″ and 2 strips 4½″ × 52¾″ on the lengthwise grain.

Binding:

Cut 7 strips 1¼″ × width of fabric.

Construction

Arrange the 3½″ × 3½″ indigo squares in various configurations to form a variety of Nine-Patch blocks. Sew the squares together in rows of 3 and press. Then sew the 3 rows together and press. Make 12.

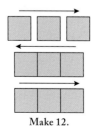

Make 12.

TIP

Pressing the seam allowances of alternating rows of blocks in opposite directions will reduce bulk.

Assembly

1. Arrange the Nine-Patch blocks, setting squares, and setting triangles in diagonal rows as shown. When satisfied with the layout, sew together in diagonal rows. Press.

Arrange blocks, setting squares, and triangles in diagonal rows.

2. Sew the diagonal rows together. Press.

3. Sew 3½" × 51½" solid indigo strips to opposite sides of the quilt. Press.

4. Sew 3½" × 44¾" solid indigo strips to the top and bottom of the quilt. Press.

5. Sew 4½" × 57½" strips to opposite sides of the quilt. Press.

6. Sew 4½" × 52¾" strips to the top and bottom of the quilt. Press.

Finishing

1. Layer and baste the quilt.

2. Quilt as desired.

3. Bind.

AN ASIAN GARDEN

Bobbi Finley, San José, California, 2010, 49˝ × 49˝;
machine quilted by Holly Casey, King City, California

Nine-Patch or *Puss in the Corner,* maker unknown, probably made in the eastern United States, c. 1830–1850, 97″ × 99″, International Quilt Study Center & Museum, University of Nebraska–Lincoln, 1997.007.0704

The Inspiration

The Irregular Nine-Patch blocks in this quilt seem to float on the pink toile background. The simplicity of the design lends itself to many interpretations, both simple and more complex. The fact that the Nine-Patches are irregular adds interest and provides a larger space in the center of the block to feature a specific fabric.

Bobbi selected a Japanese-inspired fabric with red poppies on blue circular motifs layered on a background of more circles of two-toned brown chrysanthemums. She featured this fabric in the setting squares and borders of *An Asian Garden.* The Nine-Patches with red polka dot centers are nicely balanced by the darker brown rectangles and blue corner squares, picking up the colors of the circular floral fabric. The red-striped binding adds the final touch. Though Bobbi increased the size of the Nine-Patches, she included fewer blocks, resulting in a smaller quilt.

Making the Interpretation

FINISHED BLOCK: 6″ × 6″ • **FINISHED QUILT:** 49″ × 49″

FABRIC REQUIREMENTS

Polka dot print: ½ yard for Nine-Patch centers

Brown print: ⅔ yard for Nine-Patches

Blue print: ½ yard for Nine-Patch corners

Asian print: 1¾ yards for alternate blocks, borders, and setting triangles*

Backing: 3⅓ yards

Batting: 56″ × 56″

Red striped print: ⅓ yard for ¼″-wide single-fold straight-grain binding

If fussy cutting, more will be needed depending on fabric repeat.

CUTTING

Polka dot print: Cut 25 squares 3½″ × 3½″.

Brown print: Cut 100 rectangles 2″ × 3½″.

Blue print: Cut 100 squares 2″ × 2″.

Asian print*:

Cut 2 strips 3½″ × 43″ for side borders and 2 strips 3½″ × 49″ for top and bottom borders from length of fabric.

Cut 16 squares 6½″ × 6½″. *If using a fabric with a specific motif such as the circles in Bobbi's quilt, be sure to fussy cut the squares so that the motif is in the center of the square.*

Cut 4 squares 9¾″ × 9¾″. Cut squares in half diagonally twice for setting triangles.

Cut 2 squares 5⅛″ × 5⅛″. Cut squares in half diagonally for corner triangles.

Binding/red stripe: Cut 6 strips 1¼″ × width of fabric.

Cut the border strips from the length of fabric first. Cut the squares needed from the remainder.

Construction

Blocks

1. Sew a blue square to each end of 50 of the brown rectangles. Press.

2. Using the remaining brown rectangles, sew 1 to each side of the 25 polka dot squares. Press.

3. Sew a brown/blue rectangle strip to the remaining 2 sides of each polka dot square unit. Press.

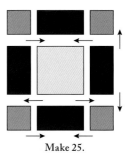

Make 25.

Assembly

TIP
Pressing the seam allowances of alternating rows of blocks in opposite directions will reduce bulk.

1. Sew the Nine-Patch blocks, alternate blocks, and setting triangles together in diagonal rows as shown. Press.

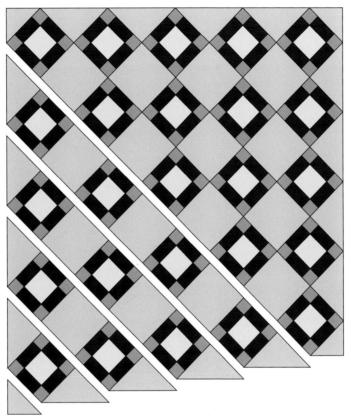

Quilt assembly diagram

2. Sew the diagonal rows together. Press.

3. Sew the 2 shorter border strips to opposite sides of the quilt. Press.

4. Sew the remaining border strips to the top and bottom of the quilt. Press.

Finishing

1. Layer and baste.

2. Quilt as desired.

3. Bind.

CONTINENTAL DRIFT

Carol Gilham Jones, Lawrence, Kansas, 2011, 37″ × 50½″;
machine quilted by Shirley Greenhoe, Thayne, Wyoming

Log Cabin Variation, maker unknown, possibly made in Indiana, c. 1910–1930, 28″ × 38″, International Quilt Study Center & Museum, University of Nebraska–Lincoln, 2000.007.0046

The Inspiration

This small Amish quilt is deeply appealing. What are the qualities that make it so attractive? Its power does not come from its size, from intrinsically interesting fabrics, or from elaborate piecing. What it does seem to come from is its unfussy, unpretentious nature. The solid, quiet colors are part of it. The limited palette is part of it. The simple Log Cabin block is part of it. But the key—the thing that makes all the elements mesh so perfectly—seems to be the improvisational look. The evidence? When Carol saw *Log Cabin Variation* on display in Lincoln, she spent long minutes looking at the quilt and making a small sketch from it. Months later, when she was still thinking of how the quilt had made her eyes dance and was considering making a quilt inspired by the Amish one, she got out the sketch and found that it was little more than a careful record of the eccentric proportions of each block. The quilt she eventually made retains the six-block and border format as well as the essential improvisational approach and rough proportions of the blocks. The grayed palette and solid-color fabrics of the Amish quilt, however, have given way to deep, saturated colors and contemporary prints, stripes, plaids, and shot cottons.

Making the Interpretation

FINISHED BLOCK:
approximately 12″ × 12″

FINISHED QUILT:
approximately 37″ × 50½″

FABRIC REQUIREMENTS

Bright colors, patterns, and values: 8 to 10 quarter-yards or fat quarters for Log Cabin blocks

Sashing: ½ yard

Border: 1¼ yards

Backing: 2⅔ yards*

Batting: 44″ × 58″

Binding: ¼ yard for ¼″-wide single-fold straight-grain binding

If your backing fabric is 44″ or wider, 1⅔ yards

IMPROVISATIONAL PIECING

Loosen up and enjoy improvisational piecing in this quilt. Rulers are optional. There is no wrong way—lines need not be straight, corners need not be square, symmetry is not in the picture and consistency is not a goal, but an assortment of interesting shapes and angles is. You are free to concentrate on pattern and color.

The one basic idea to keep in mind as you are constructing your improvisational Log Cabin blocks is this: *If you overlap 2 fabrics, both with right sides up, and cut through the 2 layers, the cut edge of 1 layer can be sewn to the cut edge of the other.* Use a rotary cutter or scissors, whichever you find to your liking.

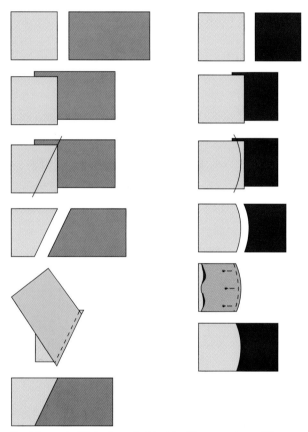

Straight cuts in fabrics layered with right sides up can be readily stitched together. Gently curved cuts in fabrics layered with right sides up will require a bit of easing as you stitch.

Construction

Log Cabin Blocks

We will walk through construction of Block A; and then, using the diagrams for Blocks B through F as references, you can take off on your own in constructing the remaining blocks. Feel free to stick closely to the diagrams or depart radically from them as you develop your own improvisational approach. Remember to layer the fabrics *right sides up* before cutting the edges that are to be sewn together.

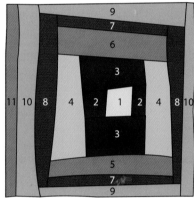

Block A with numbered assembly steps

1. For a finished block that will be approximately 12″ square, begin with a center square that is approximately 2″ × 2″.

2. Sew squares approximately 2″ × 2″ to opposite sides of the center square.

For each subsequent step, with right sides up, overlap the edges of the pieced unit and the strip to be sewn to it. Cut through both layers. Sew the cut edges together. Ends of strips that are too long get trimmed away in the next round of overlapping and cutting.

3. Sew strips approximately 2½″ × 6″ across the top and bottom of the pieced unit.

4. Sew strips approximately 2½˝ × 7˝ to opposite sides of the pieced unit.

5. Sew a strip approximately 1½˝ × 11˝ to the bottom of the pieced unit.

6. Sew a strip approximately 2˝ × 11˝ to the top of the pieced unit.

7. Sew strips approximately 1˝ × 11˝ to the top and bottom of the pieced unit.

8. Sew strips approximately 1½˝ × 12˝ to opposite sides of the pieced unit.

9. Sew strips approximately 1½˝ × 14˝ to the top and bottom of the pieced unit.

10. Sew strips approximately 1½˝ × 15˝ to opposite sides of the pieced unit.

11. Sew a strip approximately 1˝ × 15˝ to the left side of the pieced unit.

12. Using the diagrams for Blocks B through F as references, construct the remaining blocks from the centers out to the edges.

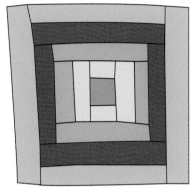

Block B

Block E

Block C

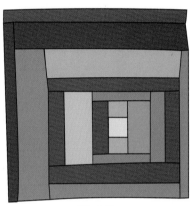

Block F

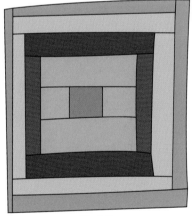

Block D

DESIGN TIP

Blocks C, E, and F appear to float because they have edge strips that are close in value to the sashing and/or border fabrics.

Assembly

1. Arrange the blocks by their letter designations.

2. For the sashing, use the same overlapping technique used in cutting pieces for the blocks. Sew strips approximately 3″ × 15″ vertically between Blocks A and F, B and E, and C and D. Trim the excess.

3. Sew strips approximately 3″ × 28″ horizontally between the pieced units. Trim the excess.

4. For the border, sew strips approximately 5½″ × 42″ to the sides.

5. Sew strips approximately 5½″ × 38″ to the top and bottom.

6. Square up your finished top, or not—suit yourself. It would be perfectly in keeping with the quirks of this design to let the edges waver and the corners stray from 90°.

D	C
E	B
F	A

Letter designations for blocks

Finishing

1. Layer and baste.

2. Quilt as desired.

3. Cut 5 strips 1¼″ × width of fabric from binding fabric. Bind.

ANOTHER INTERPRETATION

Amish Log Cabin Redux, Deb Rowden, Lawrence, Kansas, 2011, 25″ × 35″

From its striking striped border, Deb Rowden's interpretation is instantly identifiable with *Log Cabin Variation*. For the restrained solids of the Amish quilt, however, Deb substituted more boldly colored stripes, plaids, dots, and the occasional print. As a result, both the blocks and the border are quite lively. To give both design elements—blocks and borders—room to breathe, Deb bunched the Log Cabin blocks up together and refashioned the sashing of the source quilt into an inner border that separates the Log Cabin block center from the border.

PARTY IN THE DUGOUT

Carol Gilham Jones, Lawrence, Kansas, 2010, 56½″ × 56½″;
machine quilted by Lori Kukuk, McLouth, Kansas

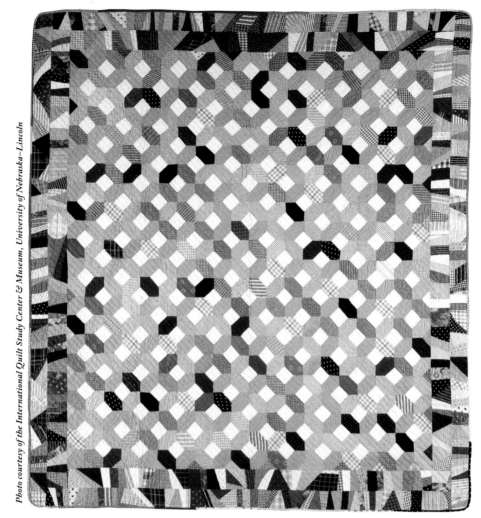

Photo courtesy of the International Quilt Study Center & Museum, University of Nebraska–Lincoln

Lattice, maker unknown, possibly made in southern Indiana, c. 1910–1930, 68″ × 75″, International Quilt Study Center & Museum, University of Nebraska–Lincoln, 1997.007.0525

The Inspiration

The imaginative maker of this quilt combined a stripped border of crazily random shapes with a highly regular center of template-cut squares and hexagons. In doing so she created a remarkable overall effect. Her lattice pattern, which pairs six-sided shapes with squares, requires a huge number of Y-seams.

Carol retained the lattice look but eliminated the Y-seams by constructing the lattice in square blocks that pair six-sided shapes with triangles. In experimenting with the square blocks on the design wall, she realized what a terrific zigzag border could be made with them. And that's what inspired her to depart from the double-stripped border of the nineteenth-century quilt. Her interpretation has a stripped inner border of irregular shapes and a zigzag outer border composed from the same square blocks as those used in the center.

The lattice pattern was called Kansas Dugout when published by Aunt Martha Studios. Made in fresh, bright batiks, Carol's Kansas Dugout quilt looks like it's hosting a party.

Making the Interpretation

FINISHED BLOCK: 4″ × 4″

FINISHED QUILT: 56½″ × 56½″

FABRIC REQUIREMENTS

Bright batiks: ⅓ yard each of 10 bright batiks

Background batik: 1½ yards

Lightweight cotton foundation fabric: 1 yard for stripped border foundation

Backing: 3¾ yards

Batting: 64″ × 64″

Binding: ⅓ yard for ⅜″-wide single-fold straight-grain binding

CUTTING

Bright batiks: Cut 152 squares 4½″ × 4½″.

Background batik: Cut 304 squares 2½″ × 2½″.

Note: In the stripped border, you will use scraps from cutting the square block pieces.

Foundation fabric: Cut 5 strips 6″ × width of fabric.

Binding: Cut 6 strips 1¼″ × width of fabric.

Construction

Square Blocks

1. With right sides together, place a 2½″ × 2½″ background square on a corner of a 4½″ × 4½″ bright square.

2. Stitch diagonally across the 2½″ square.

3. Repeat with a second 2½″ square on the opposite corner of the 4½″ square.

4. Trim ¼″ from the seams.

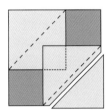

5. Press.

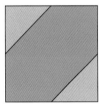

Make 152.

Inner Irregular Border

The irregular border is 4½″ × 40½″. The corner blocks are 4½″ × 4½″ square with the batik strips placed on the diagonal. Construct border strips wider than you need—in this case, 6″—and cut them to the finished size.

1. Cut the scraps of bright and background batiks into strips approximately 6″–7″ wide of varying shapes and widths.

2. Starting at one end of a foundation piece, place a batik strip right side up on the foundation and another batik strip facedown on the first strip.

3. Sew the batiks to the foundation by stitching ¼″ from the edge at the end opposite from where you began.

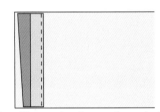

Place fabrics right sides together and stitch.

4. Press the second strip away from your starting point.

5. Repeat to make a 40½″ length.

6. Repeat Steps 2–5 to make 3 more 40½″ lengths.

7. Trim the strips to 4½″ × 40½″.

8. From the fifth strip of foundation, cut 4 squares 6″ × 6″.

9. Starting at a corner of a foundation square, place a batik strip right side up on the foundation and another batik strip facedown on the first strip.

10. Sew the batiks to the foundation strip by stitching ¼″ from the edge opposite your starting point.

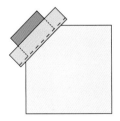

11. Press the second strip away from the corner where you began.

12. Repeat to make a square that can be trimmed to 4½″ × 4½″.

13. Repeat Steps 9–12 to make 3 more squares.

Assembly

DESIGN TIP

The Lattice/Dugout pattern has an interesting way of showing X's or O's, depending on how you look at it. To maximize the O look in this scrappy quilt, make the bright batik in each corner square point to the sides of the quilt rather than the corner. For an even greater emphasis on the O look, see the fabric placement in Georgann Eglinski's interpretation (page 56) of the IQSC&M quilt.

1. Arrange 100 square blocks in a 10 × 10 layout for the quilt center.

2. Sew the blocks together in rows. Press.

TIP

Pressing the seam allowances of alternating rows of blocks in opposite directions will reduce bulk.

3. Sew the rows together. Press.

4. Sew inner border lengths to 2 opposite sides of the center. Press.

5. Sew a corner block to each end of the 2 remaining inner border lengths. Press.

6. Sew to opposite sides of the center. Press.

7. Arrange the square blocks for the outer border.

Border assembly

8. Sew 12 square blocks in a row. Press.

9. Repeat to make 3 more outer border strips.

10. Sew outer border strips to 2 opposite sides of the quilt. Press.

11. Sew a square block to each end of the 2 remaining outer border strips. Press.

12. Sew to opposite sides of the quilt. Press.

Finishing

1. Layer and baste.

2. Quilt as desired.

3. Bind.

QUILTING TIP

Soft, curvilinear quilting lines in the dugouts make an interesting contrast with straight lines in the inner border.

ANOTHER INTERPRETATION

African Market, Georgann Eglinski, Lawrence, Kansas, 2010, 83″ × 83″;
machine quilted by Lori Kukuk, McLouth, Kansas

Georgann Eglinski also made a quilt inspired by the IQSC&M *Lattice* quilt with the loose-look border. Georgann's oranges and bold African printed cottons, large scale, and unconventional border make for a very exciting quilt. Using the same African print in four adjacent blocks, she gave her quilt strong focus by making the pattern read as a grid of O's and eliminating the play between X's and O's.

What about All Those Paired Triangles Trimmed from the Square Blocks?

If those 300-plus paired triangles cut from the corners of the square blocks are burning a hole in your scrap basket, you can remedy that problem by using almost all of them to make this charming small quilt.

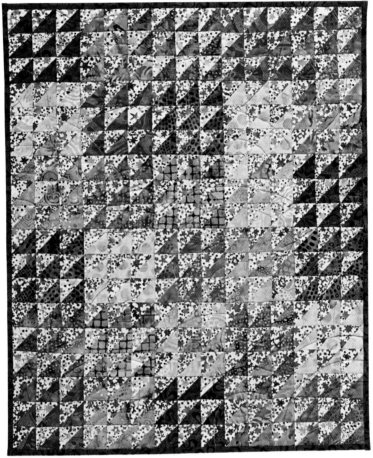

Party On, Carol Gilham Jones, Lawrence, Kansas, 2011, 19¼″ × 23″;
collection of Kathe Dougherty, Lawrence, Kansas

FINISHED BLOCK: 3¾″ × 3¾″ • **FINISHED QUILT:** 19¼″ × 23″

1. Sew the long sides of pairs of triangles together to make 270 squares. Press.

2. Group the squares by color. Sew 3 like squares in a row. Repeat to make 3 rows. Press.

3. Sew the 3 rows together into a block. Press.

4. Repeat to make 30 blocks.

5. Make a pleasing arrangement of blocks, 5 across and 6 down.

6. Sew the blocks into 6 rows, press, and sew the rows together. Press.

7. Layer and baste.

8. Quilt as desired.

9. Bind.

YIPES! STRIPES!

Bobbi Finley, San José, California, 2010, 56½″ × 56½″;
machine quilted by Holly Casey, King City, California

Log Cabin, Chimney and Cornerstone Setting, maker unknown, probably made in Ohio, c. 1880–1900, 68″ × 74″, International Quilt Study Center & Museum, University of Nebraska–Lincoln, 1997.007.0561

The Inspiration

No collection of quilts would be complete without a Log Cabin, and no group of quilts can produce a wider array of optical images through the manipulation of fabrics with different patterns or colors and the endless variations for setting the blocks together. We chose this Log Cabin in the IQSC&M collection for its more unusual block format and the great assortment of striped fabrics, which lends to the visual excitement. The blocks, when placed in this setting, produce a diamond shape containing a cross and a secondary pattern of crosses in a square. When we saw this quilt on a visit to the IQSC&M, it became apparent that this anonymous quiltmaker had a great design aesthetic. She cut many of her pieces on the diagonal to achieve a sense of movement in this quilt, perhaps influenced by some of the wool challis and delaine fabrics that were actually printed on the diagonal.

Bobbi's interpretation retains the red center square, sometimes referred to as the hearth representing the warm center of a log cabin home. The blocks in the IQSC&M quilt measure about 4½″ square, making the logs only ½″ wide. For ease of cutting and sewing, Bobbi scaled up the blocks and made fewer of them. Following the lead of the unknown quiltmaker, she selected many wildly striped fabrics and other geometric prints in a range of colors, including the dominant orange and blue stripes that make the inspiration quilt so exciting.

Making the Interpretation

FINISHED BLOCK: 7″ × 7″

FINISHED QUILT: 56½″ × 56½″

FABRIC REQUIREMENTS

Red plaid: ¼ yard for centers

Light prints: 4–6 fat quarters

Medium brown stripes and dotted prints: 4–6 fat quarters

Aqua/white stripe: ¾ yard

Blue/red stripe: ¼ yard

Orange stripe: 1 yard

Purple stripe: ½ yard

Blue stripe: ½ yard

Black geometric print: ½ yard

Black dotted print: ½ yard

Backing: 3¾ yards

Batting: 64″ × 64″

Binding: ⅓ yard for ¼″-wide single-fold straight-grain binding

First, cut each fabric (except backing and binding) into 1½″ strips. Then cut the strips in the required sizes as follows:

Red plaid: Cut 64 squares 1½″ × 1½″.

Light fat quarters: Cut 64 squares 1½″ × 1½″ and 64 rectangles 1½″ × 2½″.

Medium brown fat quarters: Cut 63 rectangles 1½″ × 2½″, 63 rectangles 1½″ × 3½″, 16 rectangles 1½″ × 4½″, and 16 rectangles 1½″ × 5½″.

Aqua/white stripe: Cut 64 rectangles 1½″ × 3½″ and 64 rectangles 1½″ × 4½″.

Blue/red stripe: Cut 1 rectangle 1½″ × 2½″, 1 rectangle 1½″ × 3½″, 12 rectangles 1½″ × 4½″, and 12 rectangles 1½″ × 5½″.

Orange stripe: Cut 64 rectangles 1½″ × 5½″ and 64 rectangles 1½″ × 6½″.

Purple stripe: Cut 8 rectangles 1½″ × 4½″, 8 rectangles 1½″ × 5½″, 17 rectangles 1½″ × 6½″, and 17 rectangles 1½″ × 7½″.

Blue stripe: Cut 1 rectangle 1½″ × 4½″, 1 rectangle 1½″ × 5½″, 17 rectangles 1½″ × 6½″, and 17 rectangles 1½″ × 7½″.

Black geometric print: Cut 14 rectangles 1½″ × 4½″, 14 rectangles 1½″ × 5½″, 15 rectangles 1½″ × 6½″, and 15 rectangles 1½″ × 7½″.

Black dotted print: Cut 13 rectangles 1½″ × 4½″, 13 rectangles 1½″ × 5½″, 15 rectangles 1½″ × 6½″, and 15 rectangles 1½″ × 7½″.

Binding: Cut 6 strips 1¼″ × width of fabric.

Construction

Press after sewing each log to the block.

Block Centers

Note: The red center, the aqua/white stripe, and the orange stripe fabrics are the same in each block. The logs surrounding the red center and opposite the aqua/white and orange stripe fabrics are selected in pairs (1 and 2, 3 and 4, 7 and 8, 11 and 12) and placed in a random manner.

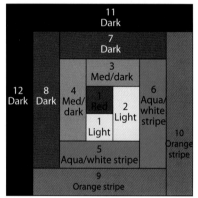

Piecing diagram; numbers indicate sewing order.

1. Sew a red square to a light square.

2. Sew a light 1½″ × 2½″ rectangle (strip 2) to the right side of the previous unit.

3. Sew a medium brown 1½″ × 2½″ rectangle (strip 3) across the top of the previous unit.

4. Sew a medium brown 1½″ × 3½″ rectangle (strip 4) to the left side of the previous unit.

You have now surrounded the red center, and the units should measure 3½″ × 3½″. We made 1 block out of the 64 total with strips 3 and 4 in the blue/red striped fabric instead of a medium brown fabric.

5. Continuing counterclockwise, sew an aqua/white striped 1½″ × 3½″ rectangle (strip 5) to the side with the light square.

6. Sew an aqua/white striped 1½″ × 4½″ rectangle (strip 6) to the side with the light rectangle.

7. Sew a brown stripe or dotted print 1½″ × 4½″ rectangle (strip 7) to a medium brown side.

8. Sew a brown stripe or dotted print 1½″ × 5½″ rectangle (strip 8) to the other medium brown side.

9. Sew an orange stripe 1½″ × 5½″ rectangle (strip 9) to a light side.

10. Sew an orange stripe 1½″ × 6½″ rectangle (strip 10) to the other light side.

The last dark rows will be completed in 4 different sets.

Block A—Purple Stripe

Make 17.

1. Sew a purple 1½″ × 6½″ rectangle (strip 11) to a dark side.

2. Sew a purple 1½″ × 7½″ rectangle (strip 12) to the other dark side.

Block B—Blue Stripe

Make 17.

1. Sew a blue 1½″ × 6½″ rectangle (strip 11) to a dark side.

2. Sew a blue 1½″ × 7½″ rectangle (strip 12) to the other dark side.

Block C—Black Geometric

Make 15.

1. Sew a black geometric 1½″ × 6½″ rectangle (strip 11) to a dark side.

2. Sew a black geometric 1½″ × 7½″ rectangle (strip 12) to the other dark side.

Block D—Black Dot

Make 15.

1. Sew a black dot 1½″ × 6½″ rectangle (strip 11) to a dark side.

2. Sew a black dot 1½″ × 7½″ rectangle (strip 12) to the other dark side.

Assembly

1. Using the diagram below and the photo of the quilt on page 58 as a guide to orientation, place the blocks in rows.

B	A	B	A	B	A	B	A
A	D	C	C	D	C	D	B
B	C	D	D	C	D	C	D
A	B	C	A	B	D	B	A
B	A	D	B	A	C	A	B
A	C	D	C	D	D	C	C
C	D	C	D	B	C	D	A
A	B	A	B	A	B	A	B

2. Sew the blocks together in rows, press, and then sew the rows together. Press.

TIP

Pressing the seam allowances of alternating rows of blocks in opposite directions will reduce bulk.

Finishing

1. Layer and baste the quilt.

2. Quilt as desired.

3. Bind.

 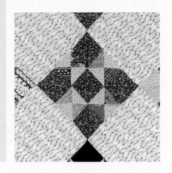

STARS AND SNIPES

Stars and Snipes, Bobbi Finley, San José, California, and Carol Gilham Jones, Lawrence, Kansas, 2011, 51½˝ × 51½˝; machine quilted by Shirley Greenhoe, Thayne, Wyoming

Variable Star,
maker unknown, United
States, c. 1850, 77˝ × 93˝,
International Quilt Study
Center & Museum,
University of Nebraska–
Lincoln, 2005.039.0004

The Inspiration

Who can resist a star quilt? Certainly not us. And not many other folks, it would seem, from
the long list of star patterns catalogued by Barbara Brackman in her *Encyclopedia of Pieced Quilt
Patterns.* Some star patterns are poetically named: Prairie Star, Star of Hope, Twinkling Star,
Harvest Star, Eastern Star, Sailor's Joy. Others have state names or biblical names, and on and
on. The pattern in this mid-nineteenth-century quilt is often called Variable Star. It is a simple
star made up entirely of squares and half-square triangles. It has a sparse, sparkling appeal to it.
The Star blocks in our inspiration quilt range from simple and crisp in two contrasting fabrics, to
somewhat scrappy, to so scrappy it is hard to find the star. The Star blocks alternate with calm,
pleasing squares of subdued stripes, all arranged in the same direction, in a soft yellow. Setting
triangles of a small print in a muted cocoa color frame the field of stars and alternating squares.

In our interpretation of the star quilt, we retained the interesting mix of staid and adventurous
elements, but we turned it topsy-turvy. Our stars are all made from only two fabrics and are,
with perhaps an exception or two, plainly read as stars. Our alternating squares and setting triangles, however, jump with life and whimsy.

Making the Interpretation

FINISHED BLOCK: *6″ × 6″* • **FINISHED QUILT:** *51½″ × 51½″*

FABRIC REQUIREMENTS

Setting squares: 1¼ yards*

Setting triangles: ¾ yard

Stars: approximately 15 fat eighths or 15 fat quarters
(Choose an interesting mix of light and dark values, stripes, dots, and several solids or prints that read almost as solids.)

Backing: 3½ yards

Batting: 59″ × 59″

Binding: ⅓ yard for ¼″-wide single-fold straight-grain binding

*More fabric will be needed if fussy cutting, depending on repeat.

CUTTING

Setting squares:
Cut 36 squares 6½″ × 6½″.

Setting triangles:
Cut 5 squares 9¾″ × 9¾″; cut squares in half diagonally twice for side setting triangles.

Cut 2 squares 5⅛″ × 5⅛″; cut squares in half diagonally once for corner setting triangles.

Star fabric: For each of the 25 stars:

Cut 1 square 2½″ × 2½″.

Cut 2 squares 3¼″ × 3¼″; cut squares in half diagonally twice.

Star background fabric: For each of the 25 stars:

Cut 4 squares 2½″ × 2½″.

Cut 2 squares 3¼″ × 3¼″; cut squares in half diagonally twice.

Binding:
Cut 6 strips 1¼″ × width of fabric.

Construction

Star Blocks

1. Sew the short sides of 8 star fabric triangles to the short sides of 8 star background fabric triangles. Press. You will have 8 pieced triangles.

2. Pair 2 triangles with opposing fabrics together along the long side. Repeat with the remaining triangles for 1 star.

3. Match the seams and sew the long sides of the pieced triangles together to form 4 squares. Press.

4. Sew the pieced squares, star square, and background squares together in rows of 3 as shown. Press.

5. Sew the 3 rows together to form 1 block. Press.

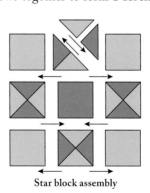

Star block assembly

6. Make a total of 25 Star blocks.

Assembly

1. Sew the setting triangles, setting squares, and Star blocks together in diagonal rows as shown. Press.

Quilt assembly diagram

2. Sew the diagonal rows together. Press.

TIP

Pressing the seam allowances of alternating rows of blocks in opposite directions will reduce bulk.

Finishing

1. Layer and baste.

2. Quilt as desired.

QUILTING TIP

Notice how the quilting brings out features of the whimsical birds in the setting squares.

3. Bind.

VIBRANT LADY

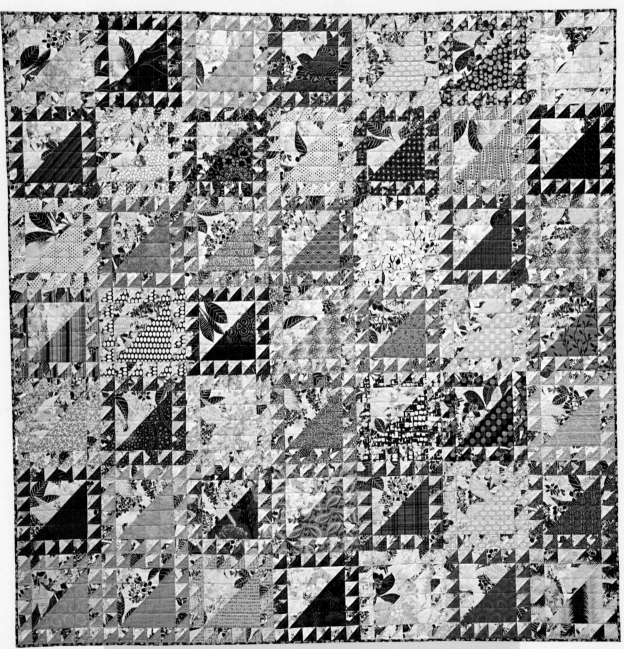

Bobbi Finley, San José, California, and Carol Gilham Jones, Lawrence, Kansas,
2011, 63½″ × 63½″; machine quilted by Lori Kukuk, McLouth, Kansas

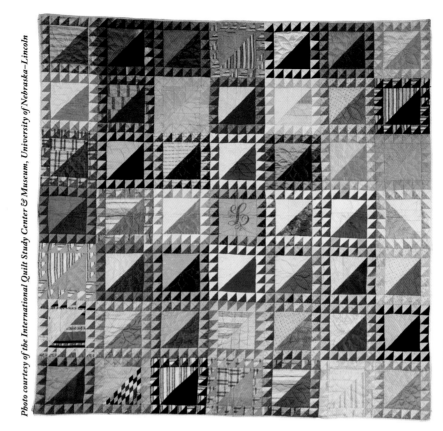

Photo courtesy of the International Quilt Study Center & Museum, University of Nebraska–Lincoln

Framed Half-Square Triangles, **maker unknown, United States, c. 1880–1900, 73˝ × 73˝, International Quilt Study Center & Museum, University of Nebraska–Lincoln, 1997.007.0430**

The Inspiration

The IQSC&M does not actually call this quilt *Framed Half-Square Triangles.* We used that name because the IQSC&M refers to the pattern as Brackman #2183, which is the Nancy Page pattern, Framed Squares. In this case, the frame—made up of twenty half-square triangle units—surrounds a square divided diagonally into half-square triangles. In this formulation the block is sometimes called Lady of the Lake. The arrangement of light and dark values within the block of this IQSC&M quilt, however, differs from the usual arrangement. Typically, the edges of the small triangle units and the large triangle unit that share a seam also share a value; the large dark triangle looks as if it has dark sawteeth. Following her own aesthetic star, our quiltmaker arranged her blocks so that the edges of the small triangle units and the large triangle unit that share a seam have opposite values. As a result, the dark and light areas of her blocks are less concentrated and more fragmented than the strong, contiguous dark and light areas of a typical Lady of the Lake block. The play of positive–negative is more lacy than forceful, which works beautifully with the brilliantly colored silks she used.

We loved the punch of the colors, but rather than using silk, we turned to contemporary printed cotton for our palette. For the upper triangle in *all* the units, we chose a floral print with a sizable repeat that includes many varied elements in light, medium, and dark values. The large size of the repeat guarantees that our large floral triangles will have many very different looks. We paired the floral print with pinks—from bubble gum to raspberry—limy greens, creams, tans, and browns. For some blocks we chose pairings with low contrast; for others we chose pairings with greater contrast. To impose a bit of order on these diverse blocks and to convey a sense of movement, we arranged them in diagonal lines, alternating low and high contrast.

Making the Interpretation

FINISHED BLOCK: 9″ × 9″ • **FINISHED QUILT:** 63½″ × 63½″

An Ideal Collaborative Project

Vibrant Lady is an ideal collaborative project for several reasons. First, having identical blocks with substantial quantities of the floral print in each ensures a certain homogeneity and harmony among blocks made by more than one person. Second, making two blocks from the same fabrics at the same time is time and fabric efficient. A fat quarter easily provides the elements of two blocks: 2 large half-square triangles and 40 small half-square triangles. And the Grid Method (page 69) for making the small half-square triangles yields exactly 40.

We chose our floral focus fabric together and then, independently of one another, made 50 blocks apiece, 2 blocks from each fabric combination—enough blocks for a complete quilt with an extra for making any color or value adjustments. We each kept 25 of our own blocks and gave the duplicates to the other with the intention of making two quilts. We loved the results and were convinced, what with Carol's plunge into pinkness being so nicely tempered by Bobbi's greens and browns and tans, that our collaborative design was better than separately designed quilts might have been.

The fabric requirements and cutting instructions are for making 50 blocks, 2 blocks from each fabric combination. If you want to make this a collaborative project, you can exchange your duplicate blocks for someone else's. If you want to make this project on your own rather than collaborate, you will still have plenty of visual variety with your 50 blocks in 25 different fabric combinations.

FABRIC REQUIREMENTS

Floral print: 4 yards

Other fabrics: 25 fat quarters, 13 light to medium-light and 12 medium to dark

Backing: 4⅛ yards

Batting: 71″ × 71″

Binding: ⅓ yard for ¼″-wide single-fold straight-grain binding

CUTTING

Note: The cutting instructions for the small half-square triangles are based on a grid method for sewing and cutting half-square triangle units that was created by both Barbara Johannah and Ernest Haight independently in the early 1970s and is described in C&T Publishing's All-in-One Quilter's Reference Tool, Harriet Hargrave, Sharyn Craig, Alex Anderson, and Liz Aneloski, 2004. See the step-by-step directions for the Grid Method (page 69). If you prefer another method for making half-square triangle units, adjust your fabric cutting accordingly.

Floral print:
Cut 25 squares 6⅞″ × 6⅞″; cut the squares in half diagonally.

Cut 25 rectangles 11″ × 13″.

From *each* fat quarter:
Cut 1 square 6⅞″ × 6⅞″; cut the square in half diagonally.

Cut 1 rectangle 11″ × 13″.

Binding:
Cut 7 strips 1¼″ × width of fabric.

GRID METHOD FOR HALF-SQUARE TRIANGLE UNITS

1. Place an 11″ × 13″ rectangle of floral fabric and an 11″ × 13″ rectangle of other fabric right sides together.

2. Draw 5 parallel lines on the fabric 2⅜″ apart down the length of the rectangle.

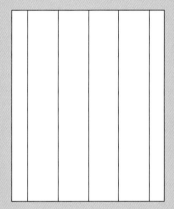

3. Using a square ruler to ensure that the horizontal lines are perpendicular to the longer vertical lines, draw 6 parallel lines on the fabric 2⅜″ apart the width of the rectangle as shown.

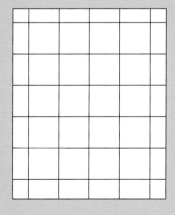

4. Starting in one corner, draw diagonal lines through every other diagonal row of squares.

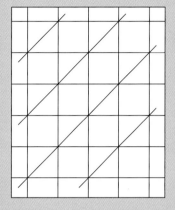

5. Draw 4 diagonal lines in the opposite direction through the empty squares.

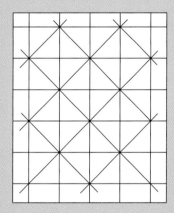

6. Pin in each triangle as shown.

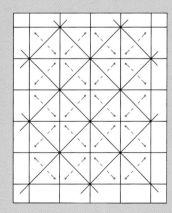

7. Starting in the bottom right-hand corner, stitch in one continuous line ¼″ from the drawn lines, turning the fabric only when you reach the edge of the grid, in the direction indicated by the arrows. Keep the same side of your presser foot toward the drawn lines at all times as you continue sewing until you have stitched on both sides of each of the diagonal lines.

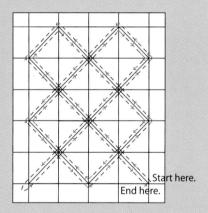

8. Cut apart on all drawn lines.

9. Press.

TIP

Press the seams of the small half-square triangle units open to reduce bulk when sewing the blocks together.

Construction

Assembly

1. Sew large floral triangles to large triangles of the other fabrics as shown. Make 2 of each fabric combination—25 pairs, or a total of 50.

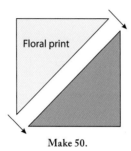

Make 50.

2. Make 40 small half-square triangle units for 2 blocks, using either the Grid Method (page 69) or a method of your choice.

3. Sew 6 units into a row. Press. Make 2.

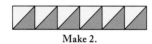

Make 2.

4. Sew 4 units into a row. Press. Make 2.

Make 2.

5. Sew the short rows to opposite sides of the block. The same fabrics should not meet along the seamline. Press.

6. Sew the long rows to the top and to the bottom of the block. Press.

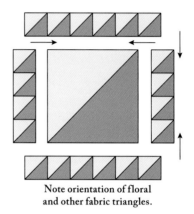

Note orientation of floral and other fabric triangles.

7. Arrange the blocks with diagonal lines of alternating low and high contrast as shown in the quilt photograph (page 66).

8. Sew the blocks together in rows. Press.

9. Sew the rows together. Press.

TIP

Pressing the seam allowances of alternating rows of blocks in opposite directions will reduce bulk.

Finishing

1. Layer and baste.

2. Quilt as desired.

3. Bind.

ANOTHER INTERPRETATION

African Market II, Georgann Eglinski, Lawrence, Kansas, 2010, 35″ × 35″;
machine quilted by Lori Kukuk, McLouth, Kansas

You may recognize the oranges and bold African-printed cottons Georgann Eglinski used in her
small interpretation of the IQSC&M's silk quilt. For the small half-square triangles, she repurposed
paired triangles cut from the corners of the square blocks in *African Market* (page 56). Georgann's
African Market II quilt, with the scrappy look of the small half-square triangles and the vitality of its
colors and large-scale prints, is quite an innovative rethinking of the classic quilt.

QUIRKY STAR

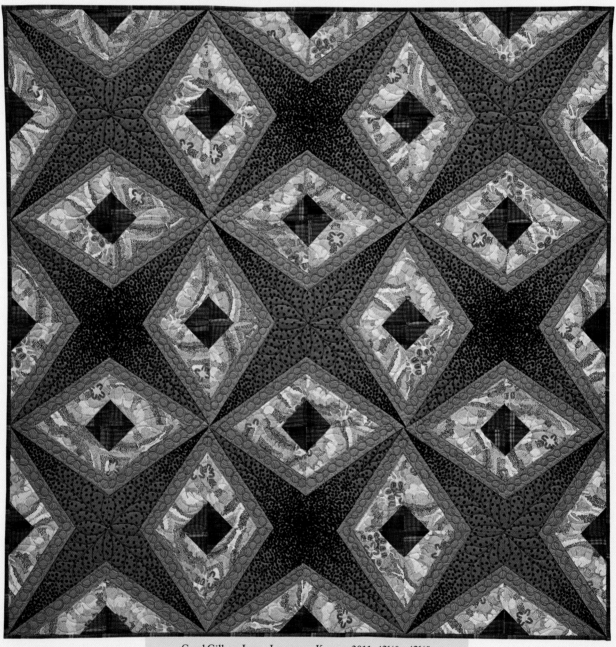

Carol Gilham Jones, Lawrence, Kansas, 2011, 42½˝ × 42½˝;
machine quilted by Lori Kukuk, McLouth, Kansas

Photo courtesy of the International Quilt Study Center & Museum, University of Nebraska–Lincoln

Star, maker unknown,
United States, c. 1930–1940,
72˝ × 72˝, International
Quilt Study Center &
Museum, University
of Nebraska–Lincoln,
2003.003.0355

The Inspiration

This marvelous machine-pieced quilt of cotton prints and feedsacks is from the Jonathon Holstein Collection at the IQSC&M. Holstein's interest in American patchwork is in American design, particularly domestic and functional design; it is in pattern, color, and form rather than in fine fabrics and needlework skills. This quilt perfectly reflects his interests. The pattern is strong and graphic. It is constructed of asymmetrical blocks that create a dynamic overall pattern by virtue of the way they are positioned in relation to each other. The pattern also has the beguiling quality of allowing the viewer's focus to shift between four-pointed stars and concentric diamonds. The quiltmaker's use of color is an exceptionally fine application of the simple prints that were available. The choice of red for the narrow strips that define the blue and green stars and the pale outer diamonds is a handsome one. Likewise, the green eyes of the diamonds could not be more visually arresting.

Carol chose to retain the pattern exactly as it is in the IQSC&M quilt. But her interpretation of the pattern is much more formal than that of the unknown quiltmaker. Instead of a scrappy look with stars of several different fabrics (sometimes even within the same star), Carol created an entirely symmetrical quilt using only four carefully chosen fabrics. She made all the stars from one fabric, but varied them by using densely concentrated dots in the centers of some stars and in the points of the others. Even these variations are symmetrically placed in the overall design. Instead of ties to hold the quilt sandwich together as in the IQSC&M quilt, Carol's more formal quilt is elaborately quilted. And instead of the knife-edge finish of the IQSC&M quilt, Carol's is bound with the plaid she used in the eyes of the diamonds.

Making the Interpretation

FINISHED BLOCK: $7″ \times 7″$

FINISHED QUILT: $42\frac{1}{2}″ \times 42\frac{1}{2}″$

FABRIC REQUIREMENTS

Brown dot: 1⅝ yards

Raspberry: 1⅛ yards

Tan: 1⅝ yards

Plaid: ¾ yard for diamond eyes

Backing: 3 yards

Batting: $50″ \times 50″$

Binding: ¼ yard for ¼″-wide single-fold straight-grain

CUTTING

Brown dot (A): Cut 12 strips 4¼″ × width of fabric.

Raspberry (B): Cut 18 strips 2″ × width of fabric.

Tan (C): Cut 15 strips 3½″ × width of fabric.

Plaid (D): Cut 8 strips 3″ × width of fabric.

Binding: Cut 5 strips 1¼″ × width of fabric.

Construction

Assembly

1. Make 36 photocopies of the paper-piecing foundation pattern (page 77).

2. Piece the appropriate strips to the foundation patterns. *(Lighter-weight papers, such as Carol Doak's Foundation Paper by C&T Publishing, achieve the best results.)*

3. Trim.

4. Arrange the blocks in rows and sew the blocks together. Press.

TIP

Pressing the seam allowances of alternating rows of blocks in opposite directions will reduce bulk.

5. Sew the rows together. Press.

Quilt assembly diagram

6. Carefully remove the paper foundations.

Finishing

1. Layer and baste.

2. Quilt as desired.

3. Bind.

ANOTHER INTERPRETATION

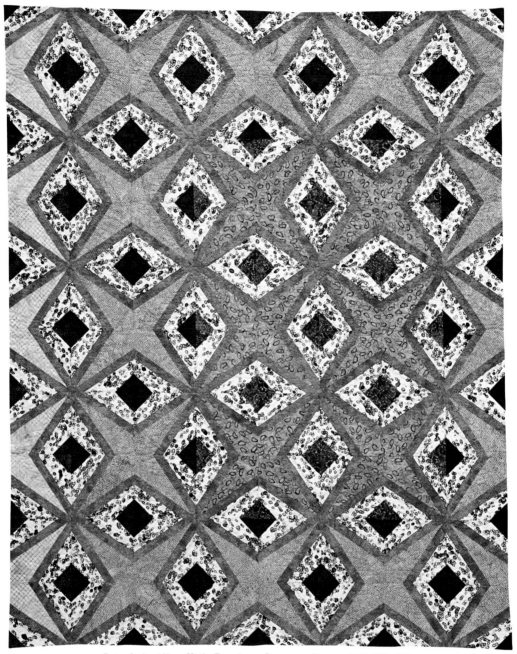

Retro Cocktail Hour, Kathe Dougherty, Lawrence, Kansas, 2011, 60″ × 75″;
machine quilted by Lori Kukuk, McLouth, Kansas

Rather than using 1930s reproduction fabrics, Kathe captured the sensibility of a more recent
bygone era by choosing batiks in somewhat subdued colors and letting the warm and cool
tones define the pattern. Her intention, as you can tell by the name of her quilt—*Retro Cocktail
Hour*—was to evoke the period of aqua Formica patterned with boomerangs.

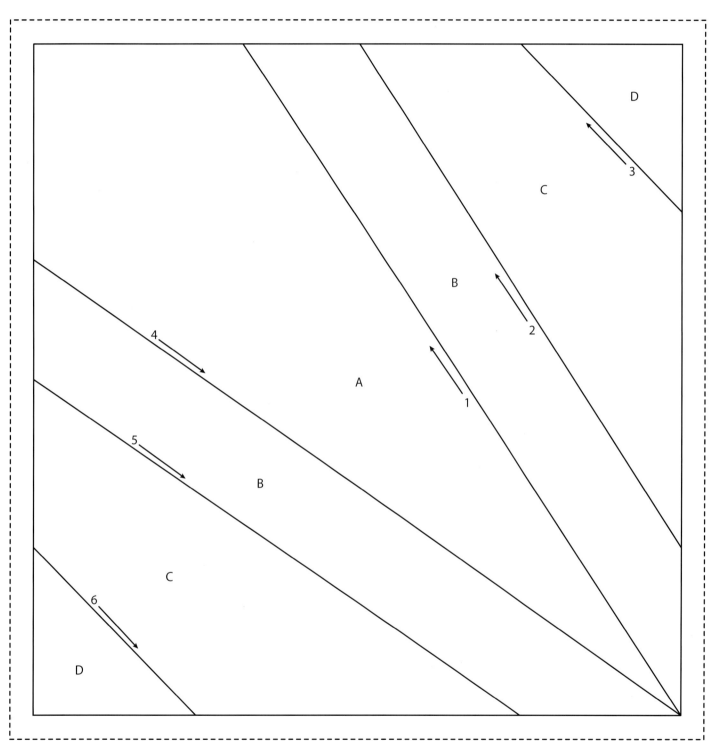

Paper-piecing pattern; stitch seams in order in direction indicated by arrows.

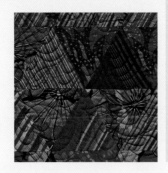

RED ROMAN STRIPES

Bobbi Finley, San José, California, and Carol Gilham Jones, Lawrence, Kansas, 2011, 52½″ × 60⅝″; machine quilted by Shirley Greenhoe, Thayne, Wyoming

••• *Fresh Perspectives* •••

Photo courtesy of the International Quilt Study Center & Museum, University of Nebraska–Lincoln

Roman Stripes, maker unknown, possibly made in Knox County, Ohio, c. 1880–1900, 63″ × 68″, International Quilt Study Center & Museum, University of Nebraska–Lincoln, 1997.007.0847

The Inspiration

We love the graphic quality of this quilt. Certainly the bold stripes against the black background are striking, and the diagonal setting of the striped equilateral triangles surely adds to the excitement. The quilt is made entirely from silk satin with narrow strips sewn together by hand to form the triangles. Wrapping around each corner of the black silk border are branches of finely embroidered flowers and leaves for added embellishment, which provide evidence of the skill of the maker.

Despite the drama of this quilt with the black background, we wanted to achieve a more contemporary look, which we believe still creates excitement. And to simplify the construction of the quilt, rather than cutting and sewing narrow strips together to create the stripes, we used a variety of printed striped fabrics in bright colors. We also swapped the black setting triangles for bold flower prints. The zigzag border adds the final touch. Visually, this quilt is not for the shy and timid.

Making the Interpretation

FINISHED QUILT: 52½″ × 60⅝″

FABRIC REQUIREMENTS

Stripes: ½ yard each of 6 different fabrics

Flower prints: ⅜ yard each of 6 different fabrics

Zigzag stripe: 2 yards for borders

Backing: 3½ yards

Batting: 60″ × 68″

Red stripe: ⅓ yard for ¼″-wide single-fold straight-grain binding

60° TRIANGLES

TIP

Placing the triangles with the stripes on the diagonal creates movement and interest in this quilt. Cutting the triangles so that the stripes are on the diagonal is a bit tricky because stripes are generally printed lengthwise on printed striped fabrics. You may have to cut lengthwise strips rather than the more usual method of cutting strips across the width of the fabric. A 60° ruler is handy for cutting the triangles, or the 60° markings on your ruler can be used. A template pattern also is provided (page 81).

Stripes: Cut 4 strips 5″ wide from each fabric with the stripes running horizontally along the length of the strip. Most likely this will be a lengthwise cut of the fabric. If the stripes do run crosswise, you will need only 2 strips from each fabric cut 5″ wide across the width of the fabric. Cut 94 triangles.

60° line

Cutting triangle using 60° mark on ruler

Floral: Cut 2 strips 5″ × width of fabric from each fabric; then cut 93 triangles.

Zigzag: Cut 2 strips 6½″ × 58″ and 2 strips 6½″ × 66″ on the *lengthwise* grain.

Note: We pieced our borders because we did not have enough of the fabulous zigzag fabric that was the perfect choice for this quilt, but the yardage stated is for borders that are not pieced.

Binding/red stripe: Cut 6 strips 1¼″ × width of fabric.

TIP

Cutting a few extra triangles will give you more design options.

Construction

Assembly

Note: Piecing 60° triangles gives you either a horizontal or vertical straight line but not both. The line in our source quilt is vertical; we liked the look of a horizontal line and oriented our interpretation that way.

1. Following the quilt photo (page 78) and the quilt assembly diagram (below), arrange the striped triangles into rows, placing the stripes on the diagonal. Note that the diagonal direction changes in each row. Triangles at the ends of the rows will be cut off after assembly.

2. Fill in the spaces with the floral triangles.

3. Sew the triangles together in rows. Press.

4. Sew the rows together. Press.

5. Trim each side: Line up the edge of the ruler with the points of the triangles and cut off the extra fabric.

Trim edges even with ruler on points of triangles.

Quilt assembly diagram

Border

Note: The zigzag pattern of the border fabric begs for a mitered border so that the lines continue around the corner without interrupting the visual impact. The following instructions are for a mitered border. Depending on your border fabric choice, you may wish to place the borders in the more usual fashion of 2 strips even with the sides, then strips across the top and bottom. Be sure to measure carefully and cut your strips accordingly if you choose the butted border style.

1. Pin the center of each side of the quilt top to the center of a border piece, and then pin the entire border in place.

2. Sew, starting and stopping the stitching ¼″ from the quilt edge.

3. Press the borders open.

4. For each corner, fold 1 border strip under so that it meets the edge of the adjoining strip and forms a 45° angle. Be sure the ends are aligned on each side.

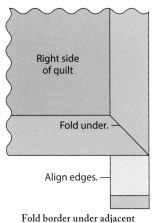

Fold border under adjacent border strip at 45° angle.

5. Firmly press the mitered fold in place.

6. Fold the quilt top diagonally from the corner, right sides together, and again align the long edges of the border strips. Draw a line on the pressed crease line. Pin across the drawn line. Beginning at the inside corner, backstitch, and stitch on the drawn line to the outside edge, and then backstitch again.

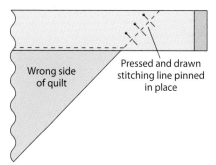

Stitching line for mitered corner

7. Turn the quilt top to the right side, and if all is well, trim off the excess fabric to a ¼″ seam allowance; press the seam open.

Finishing

1. Layer and baste the quilt.

2. Quilt as desired.

3. Bind.

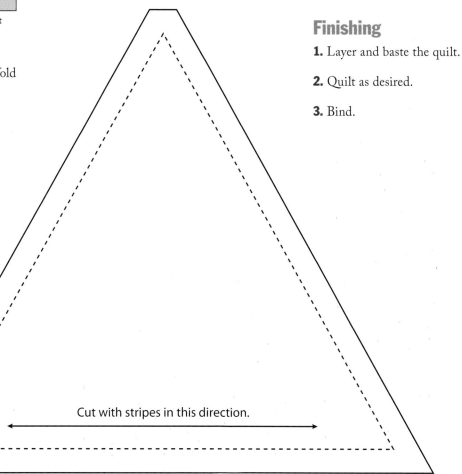

Cut with stripes in this direction.

Template pattern for 60° triangle

SPIRALS AND SPIKES

Bobbi Finley, San José, California, 1997, 52½″ × 52½″

Dogwood Blossom, maker unknown, probably made in Midwestern United States, c. 1928, 68″ × 88″, International Quilt Study Center & Museum, University of Nebraska–Lincoln, 1997.007.0851

The Inspiration

Bobbi's interest in this pattern started many years ago when she noticed it as a mystery pattern in a quilting magazine. The pattern was later identified as Dogwood Blossom, having appeared in *Capper's Weekly* magazine in 1928. The combination of the spiky arcs, running diagonally in both directions, and what appear to be Sixteen-Patches meeting in the center caught her eye. Though initially she couldn't find a dogwood blossom in the design, on closer examination she saw that the four curved sections sewn together suggest the four round petals of the blossom and the Sixteen-Patches represent the center of the blossom. She was pleased to find an example of the pattern in the IQSC&M collection. The pattern is one of several curved-seam patterns that were popular in the early twentieth century. The fabrics used in the IQSC&M quilt are poor-quality muslins, and the skill of the maker is not the highest.

Even though she pieced the spiky arcs by hand, many of the points were cut off when machine sewn to the other pieces. Still she should be commended for the boldness of her color choices and the fact that she tackled this ambitious pattern.

In her interpretation, Bobbi decided to use the spiky arcs only in the blocks on the diagonal from corner to corner and the more simple curved pieces for the arcs in the other blocks. She added interest with many circular-motif fabrics. And, unlike her 1920s predecessor, Bobbi used the modern technique of foundation paper piecing to make sewing the spiky arcs a piece of cake.

Dogwood blossom

Making the Interpretation

FINISHED BLOCK: 8″ × 8″ • FINISHED QUILT: 52½″ × 52½″

FABRIC REQUIREMENTS

Black solid: 3⅓ yards

Black print with yellow circles: ½ yard

Black dotted print: ¼ yard

Gold solid: ⅝ yard

Yellow small-texture print: ⅝ yard

Red solid: ⅔ yard

Red texture print: ⅜ yard

Red spiral print: ⅞ yard (½ yard for blocks, ⅓ yard for ¼″-wide single-fold straight-grain binding)

Backing: 3½ yards

Batting: 60″ × 60″

Binding: included in red spiral print

Optional: red yarn for spiral embroidery embellishment

CUTTING

Template patterns are on page 89.

Black solid:

Cut 36 using Template A.

Cut 72 using Template C.

Cut 10 strips 2½″ × width of fabric for the Four-Patches.

Cut 14 strips 2″ × width of fabric for piecing the spiky arcs.

Cut 5 strips 2½″ × width of fabric. Piece as needed and cut 4 strips 2½″ × 48½″ for the border.

Black print with yellow circles:

Cut 16 using Template B.

Black dotted print:

Cut 8 using Template B.

Gold solid:

Cut 2 squares 2½″ × 2½″ for corner blocks.

Cut 8 strips 2″ × width of fabric for piecing the spiky arcs.

Yellow small-texture print:

Cut 36 using Template A.

Cut 5 strips 2½″ × width of fabric for the Four-Patches.

Red solid:

Cut 2 strips 2½″ × width of fabric for the Four-Patches.

Cut 8 strips 2″ × width of fabric for piecing the spiky arcs.

Red texture print:

Cut 2 squares 2½″ × 2½″ for corner blocks.

Cut 3 strips 2½″ × width of fabric for the Four-Patches.

Red spiral print:

Cut 24 using Template B.

Cut 6 strips 1¼″ × width of fabric for binding.

Construction

Note: The 2 types of arcs to be made are the same except the curved piece in the spiky arc has the spikes and is foundation paper pieced, while in the other a simple curved piece of fabric is used. (Template B)

Spiky Arcs

1. Photocopy (or trace) the spiky arc pattern (page 89) 24 times. Cut out the paper pattern just beyond the dashed lines. *(Lighter-weight paper, such as Carol Doak's Foundation Paper by C&T Publishing, achieves the best results.)*

2. Using the 2″-wide strips, place a black solid strip and a gold or red solid strip right sides together with the colored strip on top.

3. With the printed side of the spiky arc pattern facing up, place the 2 fabrics (color on top) under the pattern with the raw edges extending at least ¼″ past the stitching line of the first point. The top of the strips should extend ½″ above the paper. Pin in place.

4. Using a short stitch length (about 20 stitches per inch), stitch on the line of the first point, beginning at the top edge of the paper, through the paper and the 2 fabrics to the bottom edge of the paper. It is important to stitch exactly on the pattern lines so that the points are sharp and perfect.

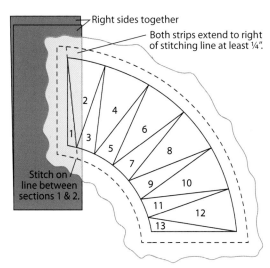

Paper piecing spiky arc

5. Turn the black fabric over and press lightly with a dry iron. Trim the top and bottom of the strips of fabric even with the edges of the paper pattern.

6. With the paper pattern facing up, place another strip of the same color right side up under the black strip, extending ¼″ to the right of the next line to be sewn and ½″ above the top of the paper pattern. Pin in place.

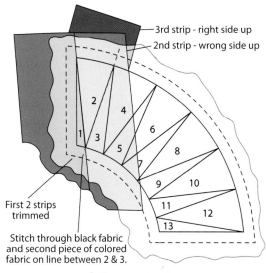

Spiky arc construction

7. Stitch through the paper and fabric on the next line as you did in Step 4. Trim the seam allowance to ¼″; then fold the colored fabric to the right and press. You now have one completed black point.

8. Continue this process from Step 4, alternating black and colored strips, until the arc is completed. Press well. Make 12 gold and 12 red.

TIP

Color placement for the spiky arc is the same for both the gold and the red blocks: The black is always in the same place; the spikes are either red or gold. However, the inner corners of the units (Template A) change colors—black in the red blocks and yellow in the gold blocks—to achieve the checkerboard center.

Gold Spiky Arc Units

1. Clip the curved seam allowance of a Template C (black solid) piece. Place a pin in the center of the curved edge and in the outer curve of the spiky arc. Place the pieces right sides together, matching the pins at the center. Line up the straight edges of the 2 pieces, place a pin at each end, and then pin the rest of the seam. With the paper side facing up, stitch on the printed seamline, sewing the 2 pieces together.

2. Repeat the process to add the Template A piece, using the yellow small-texture print fabric pieces.

3. Carefully remove the paper from the arc. Use a straight pin or tweezers to help with grabbing the paper to remove the pieces.

4. Press.

Red Spiky Arc Units

Repeat the steps in Gold Spiky Arc Units (above), using the red solid fabric instead of the gold, and the black solid fabric for Template A instead of a yellow print piece.

Curved-Piece Units

The curved-piece units are constructed as above (Gold Spiky Arc Units, Steps 1, 2, and 4), using curved pieces cut from Template B rather than the spiky arcs. As before, for the yellow units use a yellow print Template A piece, and for the red units use a black Template A piece. Use a black Template C piece for all.

Make the following curved-piece units:

16 with Template B cut from black with yellow circles

8 with Template B cut from black dotted

24 with Template B cut from red spiral

Four-Patch Blocks

1. Sew a black 2½″ strip lengthwise to each of the 5 yellow print, 3 red texture, and 2 red solid strips.

2. Press toward the black and cut into 2½″-wide segments.

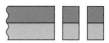

3. Sew together 2 segments with matching colors on the diagonal to make Four-Patches. Press. Each Four-Patch will have 2 squares of the same color and 2 black squares. Make the following number of Four-Patch units: 36 yellow print/black, 20 red texture/black, and 16 red solid/black.

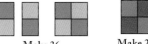

Make 36.   Make 20.   Make 16.

Block Assembly

1. Sew a yellow print/black Four-Patch to one end of each yellow arc unit (both spiky and curved), lining up the black square with the yellow print center (Template A) of the arc. Press.

2. Sew 2 units together with the arcs opposite each other, pairing 2 spiky arcs or 2 curved-piece units with the same fabrics. Press.

3. Sew a red/black Four-Patch to one end of each red arc unit (spiky arcs to red texture print, curved to either red), this time lining up the red square with the black arc center. Press.

4. Sew 2 units together with the arcs opposite each other, pairing either 2 spiky arcs or 2 curved-piece units together. Press.

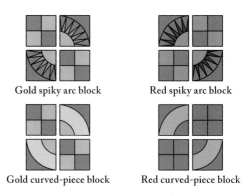

Gold spiky arc block   Red spiky arc block

Gold curved-piece block   Red curved-piece block

Assembly

TIP

Pressing the seam allowances of alternating rows of blocks in opposite directions will reduce bulk.

1. Arrange the blocks as shown in the diagram.

Blocks are identified as follows:

A. Gold spiky arc block

B. Red spiky arc block

C. Gold curved-piece block using black with yellow circle print

D. Gold curved-piece block using black dotted print

E. Red curved-piece block using red texture print

F. Red curved-piece block using red solid

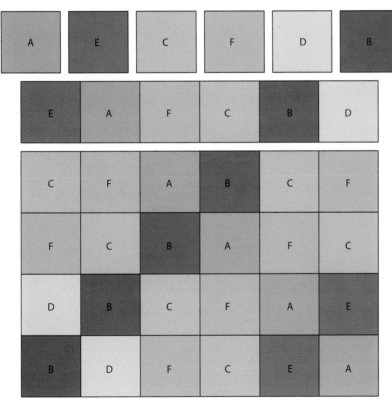

Quilt assembly diagram

2. Sew the blocks together in rows, and then press.

3. Sew the rows together. Press.

4. Sew 2½″ × 48½″ border strips to 2 opposite sides of the assembled quilt. Press.

5. Sew a 2½″ × 2½″ red texture square to one end of each of the remaining 2 border strips and a 2½″ × 2½″ gold square to the other end. Press.

6. Sew these strips to the top and bottom of the quilt, with the red squares at the red block corners and the gold squares at the gold block corners. Press.

Finishing

1. Layer and baste the quilt.

2. Quilt as desired.

3. Bind.

4. Optional: Using the red yarn, stitch spirals in the center of the black areas, including the border, as shown in the quilt photo (page 82).

ANOTHER INTERPRETATION

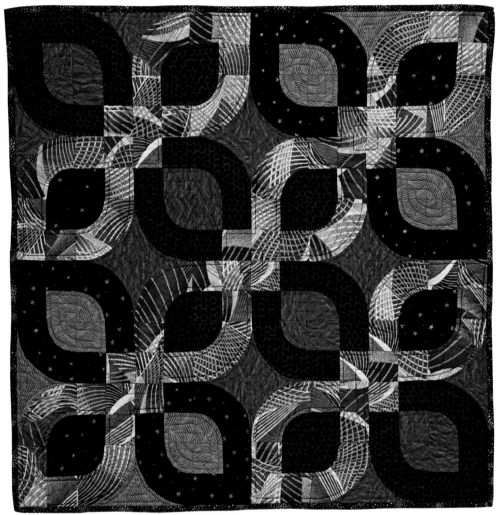

Linkage, Bobbi Finley, San José, California, 1993, 31″ × 31″;
collection of Carol Gilham Jones, Lawrence, Kansas

Bobbi's interest in this pattern also inspired her to make *Linkage,* which is simplified by replacing all the spiky arcs with curved pieces. She also manipulated the colors of the squares in the Sixteen-Patch centers to appear as Four-Patches. As a result, the pattern is opened up, elongating and connecting the arcs to travel diagonally across the quilt as uninterrupted links of ovals.

Templates

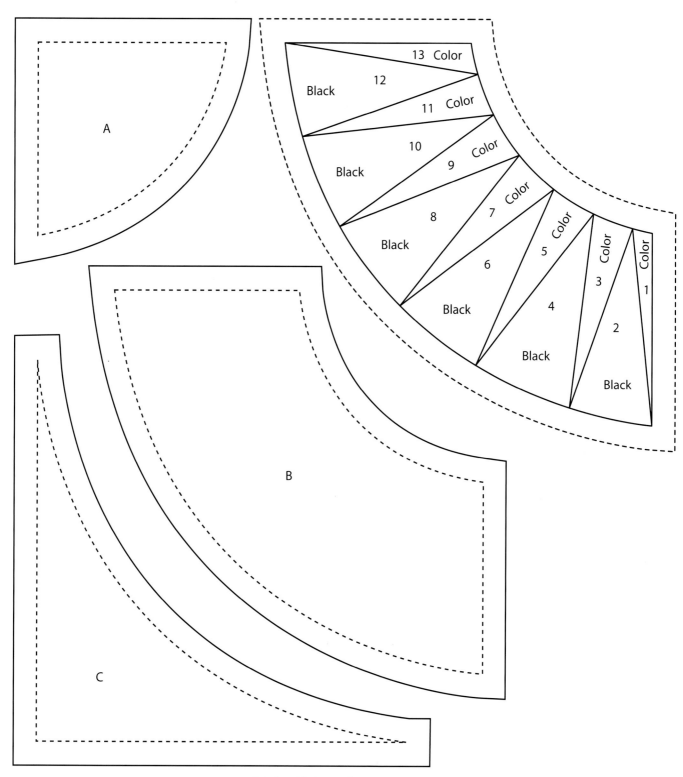

A

13 Color
12
Black
11 Color
Black
10
9 Color
8
Black
7 Color
Color
6
5 Color
Black
4
Color
3
Black
Color
2
1
Black

B

C

Spirals and Spikes template patterns

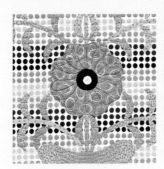 

POTS O' DOTS

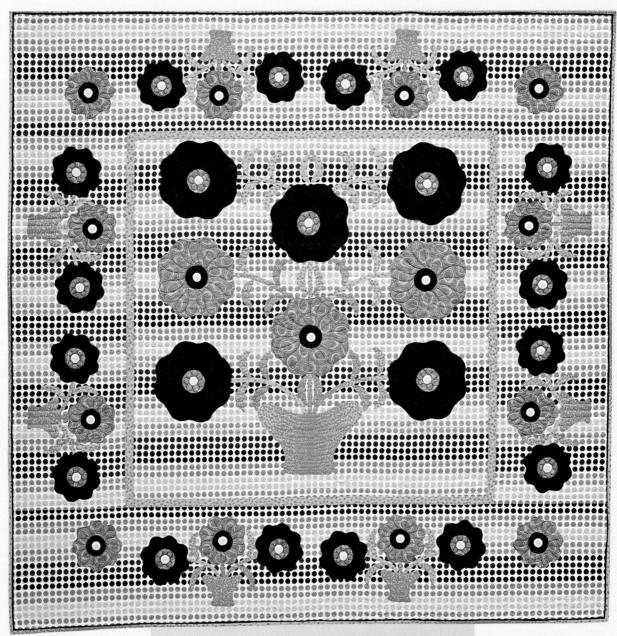

Bobbi Finley, San José, California, 2010, 50½˝ × 50½˝;
machine quilted by Shirley Greenhoe, Thayne, Wyoming

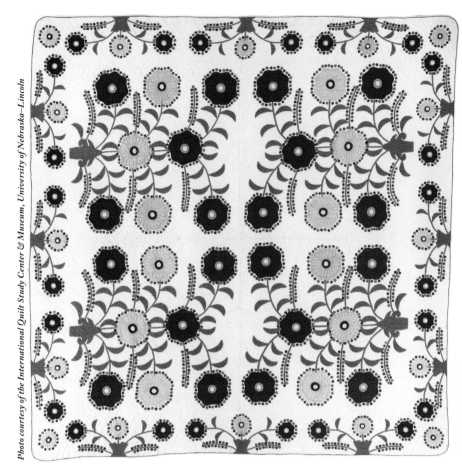

Pots of Flowers,
maker unknown,
probably made in Ohio,
c. 1850–1870, 81″ × 82″,
International Quilt Study
Center & Museum,
University of Nebraska–
Lincoln, 1997.007.0243

The Inspiration

Red and green floral appliqué quilts are a popular genre, and Ohio is considered the center of this quiltmaking tradition that began in the 1840s. The quilts are predominantly red and green on a white background, though often other colors such as orange, yellow, blue, or pink (in the case of our inspiration quilt) are added. These quilts were generally made by skilled needleworkers who often enhanced the quilts with embroidery and fine quilting designs and stitching. These quilts always seem to make a bold statement and demand attention. The delightful four-block red and green appliquéd quilt we chose for our inspiration has been published and exhibited several times, and it always catches the eye.

The large blooms (which may represent Oriental poppies) and the many stems are completely surrounded by hundreds of small berries—too many to count. Who could possibly stitch all those circles?

This is one of our favorite quilts in the IQSC&M collection, so we really wanted to include it—but neither of us wanted to stitch all those dots. And if we didn't want to, we couldn't very well encourage anyone else to do so! Choosing a polka dot fabric to imply berries for the background of the appliqués solved the problem. Bobbi also decided on just one basket of flowers for her interpretation. She redesigned the awkward-shaped pot in the original and eliminated the many horizontal stems. Two scaled-down pots fit nicely into the four borders to represent the original border design. Suggested by the colors of the dotted background fabric, the pink flowers are retained, but Bobbi chose burgundy in place of the red. She included the piping at the edge of the binding as a final finish.

Making the Interpretation

FINISHED QUILT: 50½″ × 50½″

FABRIC REQUIREMENTS

Polka dot background fabric: 2⅝ yards

Green polka dot print: 1½ yards for pots, leaves, stems, inner border, and binding

Burgundy batik or print: 1 yard for flowers and piping

Pink print: ½ yard for flowers

White solid: ¼ yard or 1 fat quarter for flower centers

Backing: 3½ yards

Batting: 58″ × 58″

CUTTING

Polka dot background fabric:

Cut 1 square 31″ × 31″ for center.

Cut 2 rectangles 13″ × 33″ on the *crosswise* grain and 2 rectangles 13″ × 53″ on the *lengthwise* grain for borders.

These pieces are oversized to allow for any shrinkage that occurs during the appliqué process. After the appliqué is completed, you will trim them to the unfinished size.

Green polka dot print:

Cut 2 strips 1¼″ × 29″ and 2 strips 1¼″ × 30½″ for inner borders.

Cut strips of 1″-wide bias to equal about 120″ for stems.

Cut 6 strips 1¼″ × width of fabric for binding.

Burgundy batik or print:

Cut 6 strips ¾″ × width of fabric.

Construction

Appliqué Templates

See appliqué template patterns on pages 95–97.

1. Trace around each template pattern on the right side of the fabric.

2. Cut out each shape adding a ⅛″ to 3⁄16″ seam allowance for turning under. Alternatively, if you prefer raw-edge machine appliqué, cut on the drawn line.

> **Green:** Cut 1 large pot, 8 small pots, 30 large leaves, and 32 small leaves.
>
> **Burgundy:** Cut 5 large flowers, 16 small flowers, 3 large circles, and 12 medium circles.
>
> **Pink:** Cut 3 large flowers, 12 small flowers, 5 large circles, and 16 medium circles.
>
> **White:** Cut 36 small circles.

Prepare Appliqué

Flowers

Appliqué the white circles to the center of the larger circles. Next, appliqué this circle unit to the center of each flower piece, pink circles to burgundy flowers, burgundy circles to pink flowers.

Stems

Fold the long edges of the green bias strips under and press to make ½″ finished bias strips or use a ½″ bias tape maker tool. Cut strips as follows:

> 2 strips 5″ long for the vertical center stems
>
> 6 strips 8″ long for the horizontal center stems
>
> 8 strips 2″ long and 16 strips 5″ long for the border

Appliqué

Center

1. Fold the appliqué background fabric in half and in half again and press to establish the center of the piece.

2. Using the photo of the quilt as a guide (page 90), place the various elements onto the background. Baste in place using thread, glue, or pins.

3. Appliqué, using your favorite method, in the following order: the stems, the pot, all the leaves, and finally the flowers.

Borders

Fold the border pieces in half to establish the center and appliqué as described above, again using the photo of the quilt as a guide for placement of the elements.

Assembly

1. Press the finished appliqué pieces facedown on a towel.

2. Trim the large center piece to 29″ × 29″.

3. Trim the 2 smaller border pieces to 10½″ × 30½″ and the 2 longer border pieces to 10½″ × 50½″.

4. Sew the green 1¼″ × 29″ border strips to the top and bottom of the center; then stitch the 2 green 1¼″ × 30½″ border strips to the sides. Press.

5. Sew the 2 shorter appliquéd borders to the left and right sides. Press.

6. Sew the 2 longer appliquéd borders to the top and bottom. Press.

Finishing

1. Quilt as desired. Shirley's quilting designs include many circles to add more dots to the theme.

Quilted circles enhance the dots of the quilt and fabric.

2. Trim away any excess batting and backing to even the quilt edges.

3. Sew the burgundy piping strips together with diagonal seams to make 4 strips each 54″ long. Press the strips in half lengthwise, wrong sides together. Pin the raw edges of the pressed piping strips to the quilt edges, lining up the edges and overlapping the strip ends at the corners. Using a long stitch, carefully machine baste the piping to the quilt top about ⅛″ from the outer edge.

4. Bind. Cut off the ends of the piping before hand stitching the binding in place on the back of the quilt.

Note: Keep the stitching straight so that the piping width is uniform.

ANOTHER INTERPRETATION

Ring around the Rosie, Helen Hodack, Los Gatos, California, 2011, 23″ diameter;
machine quilted by Annette Chavez-Fountain, Menlo Park, California

Pots of Flowers inspired Helen Hodack to make this lovely table topper. She used four pots of flowers
facing outward with two circular branches connecting the wool appliqué flowers. She loves to work
in wool appliqué. In using a cotton flannel for the background, she avoided the heavy feel of multiple
layers of wool. She also used buttons to suggest the berries in the original quilt as embellishment in the
rickrack border.

Appliqué Templates

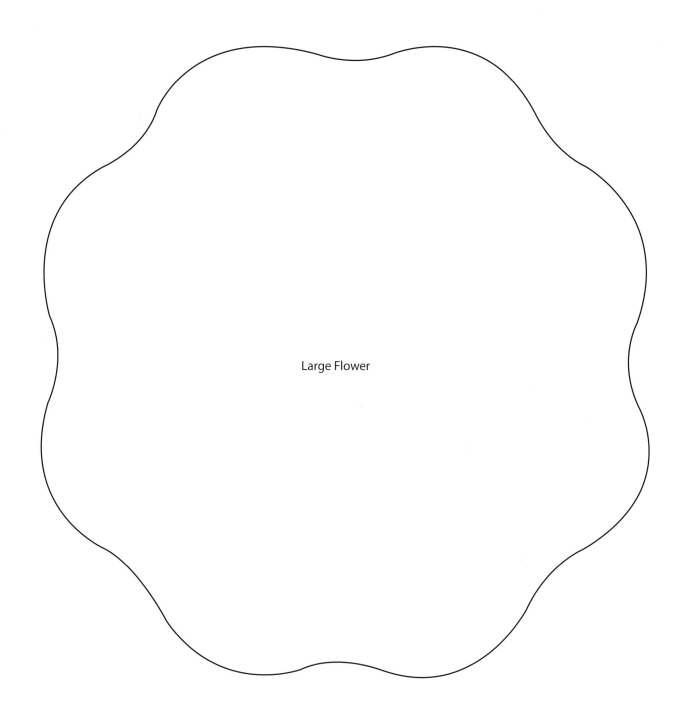

Large Flower

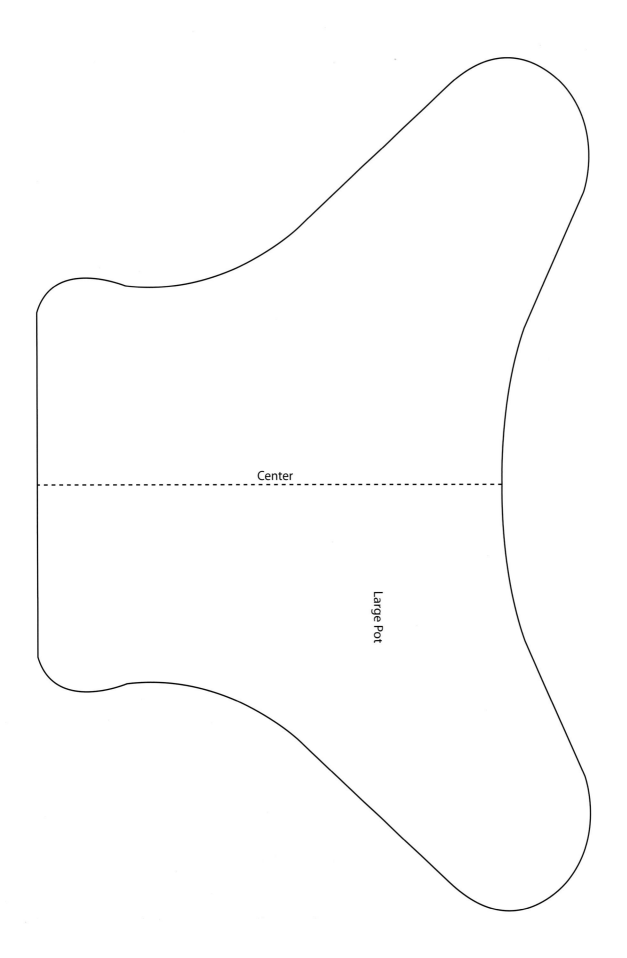

Center

Large Pot

96

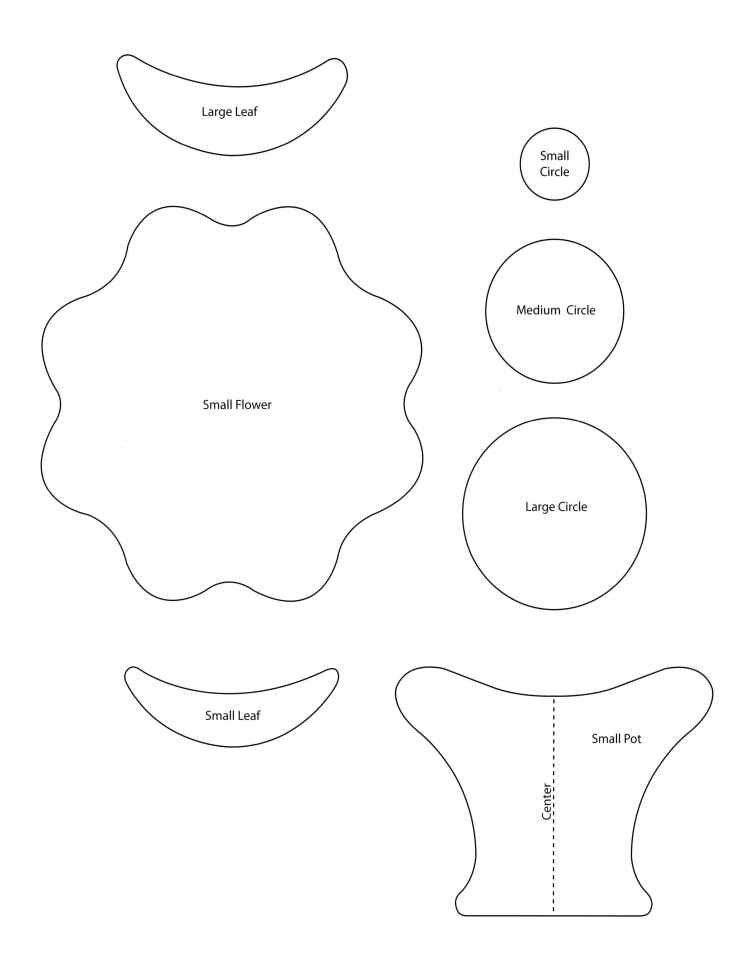

Large Leaf

Small Circle

Medium Circle

Large Circle

Small Flower

Small Leaf

Small Pot

Center

PANSY MEDALLION

Bobbi Finley, San José, California, and Carol Gilham Jones, Lawrence, Kansas, 2011, 91½″ × 91½″;
machine quilted by Shirley Greenhoe, Thayne, Wyoming

Medallion, maker unknown, possibly made in New England, 1830–1850, 107½″ × 108½″, International Quilt Study Center & Museum, University of Nebraska–Lincoln, 1997.007.0659

Making the Interpretation

FINISHED STAR BLOCK: 6″ × 6″

FINISHED QUILT: 91½″ × 91½″

FABRIC REQUIREMENTS

Light: 8¼ yards for background

Blue: 1⅔ yards for squares and rectangles and 5 stars

Reds, pinks, greens, and purples and/or blues: 9 fat quarters for stars

Large floral print: yardage that will yield 20 bouquets for cut-out chintz border

Backing: 8⅝ yards

Batting: 99″ × 99″

Binding: ½ yard for ¼″-wide single-fold straight-grain binding

The Inspiration

When we first stood in front of this quilt on a trip to Lincoln a decade ago, we did some serious hyperventilating. It is such a beauty! It is grand in scale, glorious in concept and execution. If we had been interested in replicating this quilt, the magnificence of it might have been intimidating. Our inclination, however, was to regard the early quilt as the inspirational springboard for a marvelous modern quilt with modern sensibilities. To make a more cohesive composition, we reduced the number of disparate design elements, keeping only the most appealing—the border of cut-out chintz floral arrangements, the stars, and the circular center focus. We also simplified some of the construction techniques, but did so without sacrificing the overall visual impression. For example, we replaced the truncated central star, appliquéd swags, reverse-appliquéd feathers, and scalloped border with a scheme of scattered squares and rectangles. And we replaced the 45°-diamond stars with simpler variable stars.

Note: Don't be discouraged by the length of the instructions for this quilt—it is not a difficult quilt to make. Even though it includes a number of construction steps, each step is well within the capabilities of an intermediate quiltmaker. If you take one step at a time, the quilt will come together nicely.

In keeping with the one-step-at-a-time suggestion, rather than placing all the cutting instructions at the beginning, we have grouped cutting and sewing instructions together for each component of the quilt—Star blocks, medallion center, medallion side panels, medallion corners, star border, cut-out chintz border, stairstep border, and outer border.

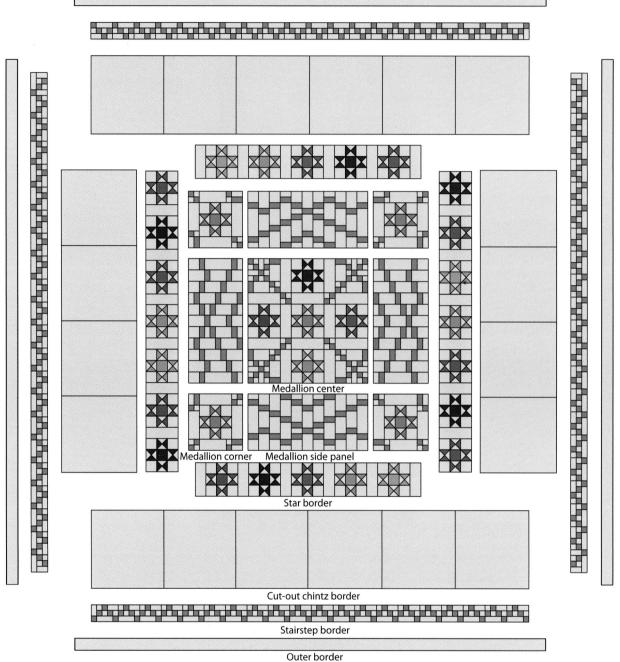

Medallion center

Medallion corner   Medallion side panel

Star border

Cut-out chintz border

Stairstep border

Outer border

Quilt components diagram

Star Blocks

This quilt has 33 stars—5 blue stars; 3 stars from each of the 9 red, pink, green, and purple/blue fat quarters; and 1 star from the fat quarter of your choice.

STAR BLOCK CUTTING

For each star:

Cut 1 square 2½″ × 2½″ from a color.

Cut 2 squares 3¼″ × 3¼″ from the same color; cut each square in half diagonally twice.

Cut 4 squares 2½″ × 2½″ from the background fabric.

Cut 2 squares 3¼″ × 3¼″ from the background fabric; cut each square in half diagonally twice.

Star Block Construction

1. Sew the short sides of the color triangles to the short sides of the background triangles. Press. You will have 8 pieced triangles.

2. Pair 2 triangles of opposing fabrics along the long side. Repeat with the 6 remaining triangles for 1 star.

3. Match the seams, and sew the long sides of the pieced triangles together to form 4 squares. Press.

4. Sew the squares together in rows of 3 as shown. Press.

5. Sew the 3 rows together to form 1 block. Press.

6. Repeat Steps 1–5 to make 33 stars total.

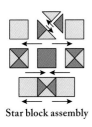

Star block assembly

Medallion

Medallion Center Construction

MEDALLION CENTER CUTTING

Blue:
Cut 3 strips 1½″ × width of fabric.

Background:
Cut 3 strips 1½″ × width of fabric.

Cut 1 strip 3½″ × width of fabric.

Cut 1 strip 6½″ × width of fabric.

Unit A

1. Sew a strip of blue lengthwise to a 1½″-wide strip of background. Press toward the blue. Repeat with a second set of the same strips.

2. Cut the pieced strips into 2½″ × 1½″ rectangles.

3. Sew the rectangles together to make 16 Four-Patches. You will have 8 rectangles left over.

Unit A; make 16.

Unit B

1. Sew a strip of blue lengthwise to a 3½″-wide strip of background. Press toward the blue.

2. Cut the pieced strip into 8 rectangles 4½″ × 2½″.

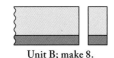

Unit B; make 8.

Unit C

1. From a 1½″ strip of background fabric, cut 8 rectangles 2½″ × 1½″.

2. Sew the 2½″ × 1½″ blue/background pieced rectangles remaining from Unit A to the background rectangles to form squares. Make 8. Press.

Unit C; make 8.

Join Units A, B, and C

Sew 3 of Unit A, 2 of Unit B, and 2 of Unit C together as shown. Make 4 blocks. Press. You will have 4 unused Four-Patches (Unit A) that will be used to assemble the medallion center.

Join Units A, B, and C. Make 4 blocks.

Unit D

From a 6½″ strip of background fabric, cut 12 rectangles 6½″ × 2½″.

Assemble the Medallion Center

1. Select 5 stars: 1 blue for the center and 4 other colors.

2. Sew the units together as shown in the quilt components diagram (page 100), using Unit D rectangles as sashing and the remaining Four-Patches as corner blocks.

Caution: Note the directionality of the corner units.

Medallion Side Panel Construction

Note: *For the sake of clarity, the instructions call for separate strips for each part of a unit and for each unit. In practice, however, you will probably wish to conserve fabric by using unused parts of strips as you assemble the units.*

MEDALLION SIDE PANEL UNIT AA CUTTING

Blue:

Cut 3 strips 1½″ × width of fabric.

Background:

Cut 2 strips 1½″ × width of fabric.

Cut 1 strip 2½″ × width of fabric.

Cut 1 strip 3½″ × width of fabric.

Unit AA

1. Sew blue and background strips together lengthwise in the following order to make a 10½″-wide strip:

> 1½″ background, 1½″ blue, 3½″ background, 1½″ blue, 1½″ background, 1½″ blue, and 2½″ background

2. Cut the pieced strip into 8 rectangles 10½″ × 2½″.

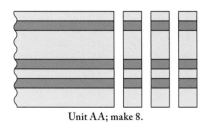

Unit AA; make 8.

MEDALLION SIDE PANEL UNIT BB CUTTING

Blue:

Cut 2 strips 1½″ × width of fabric.

Background:

Cut 1 strip 2½″ × width of fabric.

Cut 2 strips 3½″ × width of fabric.

Unit BB

1. Sew blue and background strips together lengthwise in the following order to make a 10½″-wide strip:

> 2½″ background, 1½″ blue, 3½″ background, 1½″ blue, and 3½″ background

2. Cut the pieced strip into 12 rectangles 10½″ × 2½″.

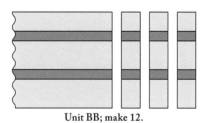

Unit BB; make 12.

MEDALLION SIDE PANEL UNIT CC CUTTING

Blue:

Cut 2 strips 1½″ × width of fabric.

Background:

Cut 1 strip 1½″ × width of fabric.

Cut 1 strip 2½″ × width of fabric.

Cut 1 strip 5½″ × width of fabric.

Unit CC

1. Sew blue and background strips together lengthwise in the following order to make a 10½″-wide strip:

> 1½″ background, 1½″ blue, 5½″ background, 1½″ blue, and 2½″ background

2. Cut the pieced strip into 8 rectangles 10½″ × 2½″.

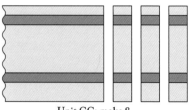

Unit CC; make 8.

MEDALLION SIDE PANEL UNIT DD CUTTING

Blue:

Cut 2 strips 1½″ × width of fabric.

Background:

Cut 1 strip 2½″ × width of fabric.

Cut 2 strips 3½″ × width of fabric.

Unit DD

1. Sew blue and background strips together lengthwise in the following order to make a 10½″-wide strip:

> 3½″ background, 1½″ blue, 3½″ background, 1½″ blue, and 2½″ background

2. Cut the pieced strip into 8 rectangles 10½″ × 2½″.

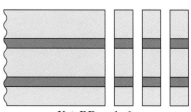

Unit DD; make 8.

Blue:

Cut 3 strips 1½″ × width of fabric.

Background:

Cut 1 strip 1½″ × width of fabric.

Cut 2 strips 3½″ × width of fabric.

Unit EE

1. Sew blue and background strips together lengthwise in the following order to make a 10½″-wide strip:

1½″ blue, 3½″ background, 1½″ blue, 3½″ background, 1½″ blue, and 1½″ background

2. Cut the pieced strip into 8 rectangles 10½″ × 2½″.

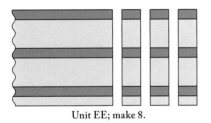

Unit EE; make 8.

Assemble the Medallion Side Panels

Sew together the side panels as shown. Make 4.

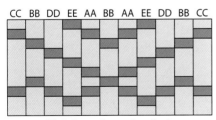

CC BB DD EE AA BB AA EE DD BB CC

Medallion side panel; make 4.

Medallion Corners Construction

Blue:

Cut 2 strips 1½″ wide × width of fabric.

Background:

Cut 3 strips 2½″ wide × width of fabric; cut the strips into 8 rectangles 6½″ × 2½″ and 8 rectangles 5½″ × 2½″.

Cut 2 strips 1½″ wide × width of fabric.

1. Sew 1½″-wide blue and background strips together lengthwise to make a 2½″-wide strip.

2. Cut the pieced strip into 24 rectangles 1½″ × 2½″.

3. Sew 16 of the pieced rectangles together to make 8 Four-Patches.

Four-Patches; make 8.

4. Sew 1 of the 8 remaining pieced rectangles to each 5½″ × 2½″ background rectangle to form a 6½″ × 2½″ rectangle.

Caution: Note the directionality of the units.

6½″ × 2½″ rectangles; make 4 of each.

5. Sew 1½″-wide blue and background strips together lengthwise to make a 2½″-wide strip.

6. Cut the pieced strip into 8 squares 2½″ × 2½″.

7. With a blue star in the center of each, assemble the medallion corners as shown.

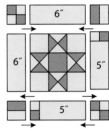

Medallion corner; make 4.

Medallion Assembly

Assemble the medallion center, side panels, and corners as shown in the Quilt Components diagram (page 100).

Caution: Note the directionality of the side panels and corners.

Borders

Star Border Construction

STAR BORDER CUTTING

Background:

Cut 4 strips 2½″ × width of fabric; cut the strips into 24 rectangles 6½″ × 2½″.

1. Make 4 rows of 5 stars each. Add sashing rectangles 6½″ × 2½″ between the stars and on each short end. Sew. Press.

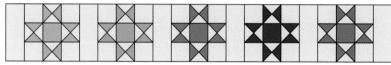

Star border; make 4.

2. Sew another star to each end of 2 of the star borders. Press.

3. Sew the 2 short star borders to 2 opposite sides of the medallion. Press.

4. Sew the 2 long star borders to the remaining sides of the medallion. Press.

Cut-Out Chintz Border Construction

CUT-OUT CHINTZ BORDER CUTTING

Background:

Cut 2 strips 14″ × 54½″ on the *lengthwise* grain.

Cut 2 strips 14″ × 81½″ on the *lengthwise* grain.

Large floral print:

Cut 20 bouquets or floral arrangements.

Note: *Either allow a generous ⅛″ outside the floral image to turn under for needle-turn appliqué or apply fusing material and cut out the finished shape for fusible appliqué. With the seam allowances stitched under, the vases of pansies we used measure 11¼″ top to bottom and 10″ at the widest point. You can use a smaller bouquet, but the border width will not accommodate one that is much larger.*

TIP

If the outline of the bouquet is more complicated than what you want to stitch or fuse, simplify it as you cut.

1. On each 54½″-long strip, position 4 bouquets with the bouquet tops toward the same long side of the strip. Bouquets on the ends should be approximately half as far from the end of the strip as the bouquets are from each other.

2. Baste and appliqué by your preferred method, or fuse the bouquets to the background fabric.

3. On each 81½″-long strip, position 6 bouquets with the bouquet tops toward the same long side of the strip. Bouquets on the ends should be approximately half as far from the end of the strip as the bouquets are from each other.

4. Baste and appliqué by your preferred method, or fuse the bouquets to the background fabric.

5. With the bouquet tops toward the medallion, sew the 54½″ strips to opposite sides of the quilt. Press.

6. With the bouquet tops toward the medallion, sew the 81½″ strips to the remaining sides. Press.

Stairstep Border Construction

STAIRSTEP BORDER CUTTING

These instructions are for 3 strip sets. If your fabric is less than 42″ wide, you will need to make 4 strip sets of each type, or use scraps from previous sections.

Blue:

Cut 12 strips 1½″ × width of fabric.

Background:

Cut 9 strips 1½″ × width of fabric.

Cut 3 strips 2½″ × width of fabric.

Cut 3 strips 3½″ × width of fabric.

1. Using the blue and background strips, make 3 identical strip sets by sewing strips together in the following order to make a 4½″-wide strip: 1½″ background, 1½″ blue, and 2½″ background. Press.

2. Using the blue and background strips, make 3 identical strip sets by sewing strips together in the following order to make a 4½″-wide strip: 1½″ blue, 1½″ background, 1½″ blue, and 1½″ background. Press.

3. Using the blue and background strips, make 3 identical strip sets by sewing strips together in the following order to make a 4½″-wide strip: 3½″ background and 1½″ blue. Then press.

4. Cut the pieced strips into 80 rectangles 1½″ × 4½″ of each type.

5. Sew 3 rectangles together to make a unit as shown. Press. Make 80 units.

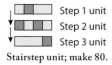

Step 1 unit
Step 2 unit
Step 3 unit

Stairstep unit; make 80.

6. Sew 20 units into a row. Press. Make 4 rows.

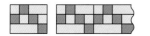

Stairstep row; make 4 with 20 units each.

7. From leftover strips, cut 4 blue squares 1½″ × 1½″ and 4 background rectangles 2½″ × 1½″. Sew squares to the short end of the rectangles to make 4 rectangles 3½″ × 1½″. Press.

8. Sew a pieced rectangle to one end of each of the 4 stairstep border sides. Press.

Note: The blue end of the rectangle added to each border side will be toward the outer edge of the quilt and will make the stairstep pattern symmetrical.

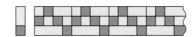

9. For the stairstep corner, use leftover 1½″ blue and background strips; follow the instructions in Medallion Center Construction, Steps 1–3 (page 101) to make 4 Four-Patches. Press.

10. Sew a 2½″ × 1½″ rectangle of background fabric to one side of each Four-Patch. Press. Sew a rectangle of background fabric 3½″ × 1½″ to an adjacent side as shown, noting the orientation of the background fabric. Press.

Stairstep border corner unit; make 4.

11. Sew the stairstep borders to the top and bottom of the quilt. Press.

12. Sew the border corners (from Step 10) onto the remaining 2 stairstep borders, placing them to continue the stairstep pattern. Press.

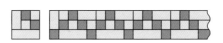

13. Sew the borders with corners on opposite sides of the quilt. Press.

Outer Border Construction

1. From the long background strips remaining from cutting the background for the bouquet border, cut long 2½″-wide strips.

2. Measure through the center of the quilt horizontally to determine the lengths of the top and bottom borders. Measure vertically and add 4½″ to determine the length of the side borders.

3. Piece the strips as necessary for length.

4. Sew the strips to the top and bottom first, and then to the sides of the quilt, pressing after each addition.

Finishing

1. Layer and baste.

2. Quilt as desired. Use quilting to bring out features of your bouquets or flower arrangements.

3. Cut 10 strips 1¼″ × width of fabric from the binding fabric. Bind.

POT OF FLOWERS MEDALLION

Carol Gilham Jones and Georgann Eglinski, Lawrence, Kansas, 2010, 88½˝ × 88½˝;
machine quilted by Shirley Greenhoe, Thayne, Wyoming

Medallion, Mary Stavely,
East Yorkshire, England, 1833,
83″ × 99″, International Quilt
Study Center & Museum,
University of Nebraska–
Lincoln, 2006.031.0001

The Inspiration

Mary Stavely was a young girl studying needlework when she embroidered the medallion of this lovely early-nineteenth-century quilt. The medallion is composed of scattered floral motifs, a lion, a ram, and a scroll inscribed with the story of Mary's handiwork. The small scale of the embroidered representations requires close inspection for appreciation. In contrast, the piecing surrounding the medallion is on a larger scale and shows well from any distance. Even so, because every other fabric in the pieced pattern is very light or white, the piecing has an airy, perforated quality that does not overwhelm the light, spare medallion. In interpreting Mary's *Medallion*, we wanted to keep the light, open look of the piecing as well as the combination of an on-point medallion and surrounding pieced blocks. We wanted to make a more balanced overall composition, and to do that, we decided to give the medallion more visual weight than the embroidered medallion has.

Georgann chose a wonderful pale but very visually exciting fabric—a large-scale leaf print in white and pastels with occasional details in stronger colors. We made the leaf print do double duty: it lightens—so much so that the stronger colors seem to float on it—and because it is in the medallion, the piecing, *and* the borders, it unifies. The leaf print has warmth to it, even though it is pastel, so we were able to pair it with coral reds for a luscious richness in the medallion and the piecing. In the piecing, we heightened the visual appeal by including some of the stronger accent colors from the leaf print. Georgann appliquéd the medallion using Bobbi's pattern from her *Pots o' Dots* (page 90). To fill the diamond space of the on-point medallion, Georgann added a flower on the top. We also made a simple adjustment to the piecing pattern to make it symmetrical.

Making the Interpretation

FINISHED BLOCK: 4″ × 4″ • **FINISHED QUILT:** 88½″ × 88½″

FABRIC REQUIREMENTS

Light: 6½ yards if your light fabric is directional, or 5⅛ yards if your fabric is multidirectional, for background and borders

Reds: 11 quarter-yards or fat quarters for squares, half-square triangle blocks, flowers, and flowerpot

Accent colors (golden yellows, pinks, yellow-greens, aquas/turquoises): variety of quarter-yards, fat quarters, or scraps to total 1 yard for accent squares

Green or blue-green (medium to dark value): ½ yard or 2 fat quarters for stems and leaves

Backing: 8⅜ yards

Batting: 96″ × 96″

Binding: ½ yard for ¼″-wide single-fold straight-grain binding

CUTTING

Light:

Cut 68 squares 4⅞″ × 4⅞″; cut each square in half diagonally.

Cut 2 squares 8⅞″ × 8⅞″; cut each square in half diagonally.

Cut 4 strips 8½″ × 80½″ on the *lengthwise* grain.

Reds:

Cut 68 squares 4½″ × 4½″.

Cut 52 squares 4⅞″ × 4⅞″; cut each square in half diagonally.

Accent colors:

Cut 56 squares 4½″ × 4½″.

Binding:

Cut 10 strips 1¼″ × width of fabric.

Construction

Medallion

Background

1. The finished on-point medallion is 48″ top to bottom and side to side, wider than standard 42″ quilting cotton. To keep this diagonal on the straight grain of the fabric, piece the medallion background as shown:

If your light fabric is obviously directional, as ours is, cut 4 squares 26″ × 26″ in half diagonally. Using the same half-square triangle from each square, arrange them into a square, and sew them together.

If your light fabric is multidirectional, cut 2 squares 26″ × 26″ in half diagonally. Arrange the triangles into a square and sew them together.

2. Press the seams open.

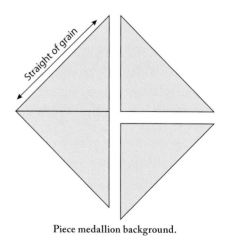

Piece medallion background.

Appliqué

1. Using *Pot o' Dots* templates (patterns, pages 95–97), cut 9 red Large Flowers, 9 gold Large Circles, and 9 turquoise Small Circles.

Cut 1 Large Pot from a red or red/turquoise fabric.

Cut 30 green or blue-green pieces using the Large Leaf template pattern and enough 1˝-wide bias strips to equal 48˝ in length for stems. Trim the finished bias strips as follows:

> 3 strips 4˝ long for the vertical stems

> 6 strips 6˝ long for the horizontal stems

2. Refer to Prepare Appliqué (page 92) and Appliqué (page 93) for preparing and stitching the pot of flowers.

3. Press the finished appliqué pieces facedown on a towel, and trim to 34˝ × 34˝.

Assembly

Piecing

1. Pair each red triangle with a light triangle.

2. Sew the long sides together to make 104 squares 4½˝ × 4½˝. Press.

3. Arrange a quarter of the accent-color squares (14), pieced squares (26), red squares (17), and light triangles (8) as shown.

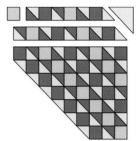

Place accent-color squares as shown.

4. Sew the squares together in rows, press, and sew the rows together, reserving the large light triangle for last. Press.

5. Repeat Steps 3 and 4 to make 4 sections.

6. Sew the long diagonal side of a pieced section to one side of the medallion, beginning and ending the seam with a lockstitch ¼˝ from each end. Press.

7. Repeat for each side of the medallion.

8. With right sides together, fold the medallion in half from one point to the opposite point. Align the edges of the pieced sections on one end of the folded medallion. Starting at the outside edge, join the pieced sections by sewing toward the medallion. End the seam with a lock stitch ¼˝ from the end. Press.

9. Repeat for each Y-seam.

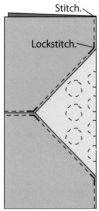

Sew from the outer edges toward medallion.

Borders

1. Sew a border length, which will be longer than the quilt edge, to one edge of the quilt, starting with the ends of the 2 pieces together and ending with a lockstitch ¼˝ from the other end of the quilt edge. Approximately 8˝ of the border length will be loose and extend beyond the quilt edge. Press.

2. Sew another border length to the long side created by the first border length being sewn to the quilt. Press.

3. Repeat for the third side. Press.

4. Repeat for the fourth side; then sew the short end of the fourth border length to the loose part of the first border length that extends beyond the quilt edge, lockstitching at the beginning. Press.

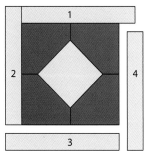

Sew borders in order.

Finishing

1. Layer and baste.

2. Quilt as desired.

3. Bind. We bound the quilt with the light leaf print to extend the floating effect all the way to the edges.

QUILTING TIP

Shirley Greenhoe's fluid quilting glides right over the appliqué, perfectly balancing the visual significance of the piecing and the appliqué as intended. Shirley designed a quilting pattern for the piecing that underscores the concentric diamonds expanding out from the medallion. The pattern with which she quilted the diamonds formed by red squares and light triangles is quite different from the pattern in the diamonds formed by accent-color squares and red triangles.

ABOUT THE AUTHORS

Photo by Deb Rowden

Carol Gilham Jones and Bobbi Finley

Carol Gilham Jones lives in Lawrence, Kansas, with her sweetheart, Charles, and their dogs, Sumo and Grace. Bobbi Finley lives in San José, California, with her cat, Thomas, near her son and daughter-in-law, Todd and Kimberly. Bobbi and Carol had the good fortune of meeting at a San Francisco Bay Area quilting retreat in 1990. The friendship that grew out of their meeting soon included working together on quilts, despite their geographic distance. After collaborating on many quilt projects over the years, they wrote their first book together, *Tile Quilt Revival: Reinventing a Forgotten Form*, which was published by C&T Publishing in 2010. And now, reinventing again, they offer this book, their latest collaboration.

Bobbi is pleased to have one of her quilts in the collection of the American Museum of Folk Art in New York and feels fortunate that her quilts have been recognized in books and exhibits. Her love for exploring the history of quilts and their makers has led her to actively participate in the American Quilt Study Group, serving as a board member and former coordinator of the study quilt exhibits.

Carol's quilts have twice appeared on the cover of the magazine *Quilters Newsletter* and in many other publications, including Judi Warren Blaydon's *Collage+Cloth=Quilt*, published by C&T Publishing in 2010. In 2004 and 2005, a quilt Carol made with Bobbi and Georgann Eglinski traveled throughout Japan in the exhibition *Japanese Imagery in One Hundred Quilts*, which featured the work of 75 artists from Japan and 25 from other countries.

PREVIOUS BOOK BY AUTHORS:

Great Titles *from* C&T PUBLISHING

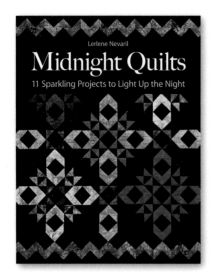

Lerlene Nevaril

Midnight Quilts

11 Sparkling Projects to Light Up the Night

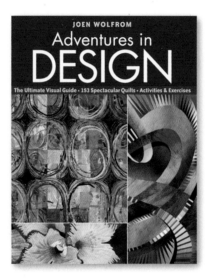

JOEN WOLFROM

Adventures in DESIGN

The Ultimate Visual Guide • 153 Spectacular Quilts • Activities & Exercises

Charlotte Warr Andersen

Bonus! Free Inch! Ruler Tape

One Line at a Time, Encore

35 NEW GEOMETRIC MACHINE-QUILTING DESIGNS

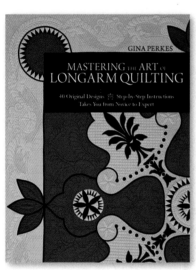

GINA PERKES

MASTERING THE **ART** OF **LONGARM QUILTING**

40 Original Designs ✿ Step-by-Step Instructions
Takes You from Novice to Expert

NEW ENGLISH PAPER PIECING

A Faster Approach to a Traditional Favourite • 10 Quilted Projects

SUE DALEY

Weeks Ringle and Bill Kerr

TRANSPARENCY QUILTS

10 Modern Projects
Keys for Success in Fabric Selection
From the Modern Quilt Studio

Available at your local retailer or **www.ctpub.com** *or* **800-284-1114**

For a list of other fine books from C&T Publishing, visit our website
to view our catalog online.

C&T PUBLISHING, INC.

P.O. Box 1456
Lafayette, CA 94549
800-284-1114

Email: ctinfo@ctpub.com
Website: www.ctpub.com

C&T Publishing's professional photography services are now available
to the public. Visit us at www.ctmediaservices.com.

Tips and Techniques can be found at www.ctpub.com >
Consumer Resources > Quiltmaking Basics > Tips & Techniques for
Quiltmaking & More

For quilting supplies:

COTTON PATCH

1025 Brown Ave.
Lafayette, CA 94549
Store: 925-284-1177
Mail order: 925-283-7883

Email: CottonPa@aol.com
Website: www.quiltusa.com

Note: Fabrics shown may not be currently available, as fabric
manufacturers keep most fabrics in print for only a short time.